JAMES JOYCE

PETER COSTELLO

GILL & MACMILLAN

Gill & Macmillan Ltd
Goldenbridge
Dublin 8
with associated companies throughout the world
© Peter Costello 1980, 1998
0 7171 2687 0
First published 1980 in the Gill's Irish Lives series
Printed in Malaysia

A catalogue record is available for this book
from the British Library.

1 3 5 4 2

For Timothy

Contents

Acknowledgments   vii

Introduction   1

1. Childhood and Youth   6

2. Student Days   17

3. Going into Exile   29

4. Trieste   41

5. Crisis   51

6. The Tide Turns   61

7. *Ulysses*   73

8. Paris: Work in Progress   84

9. *Finnegans Wake*   95

10. Joyce the Writer   105

11. Final Years   114

12. Epilogue: Joyce's Dublin   125

Bibliography   130

Index   133

Acknowledgments

The author and publisher wish to acknowledge the permission of the Society of Authors as the literary representatives of the estate of James Joyce, and of the following publishers to quote from the works of James Joyce: Jonathan Cape (*Chamber Music, Dubliners,* and *A Portrait of the Artist as a Young Man*); The Bodley Head (*Ulysses*); Faber and Faber (*Finnegans Wake, Pomes Penyeach*); The Viking Press (*Chamber Music, Dubliners, A Portrait of the Artist as a Young Man, Pomes Penyeach, Finnegans Wake*); and Random House (*Ulysses*).

Introduction

When James Joyce died in Zurich in January 1941 he left behind an enduring literary legend.

His life of exile, poverty and pain had become common knowledge. His books, though largely unread, were notorious for their veiled obscurity and supposed obscenity: Joyce put into print words which had long lived only from mouth to mouth. Actions and thoughts often considered unfit to be read about were an integral part of his novels. But Joyce was more than just obscene: he was known to be difficult. His frankness served an uncompromising literary ideal derived from the philosophies of Aristotle and Aquinas. What he wrote was not cheap smut for schoolboys. Though he wrote about the lives of ordinary Dublin people, the way he wrote about them was extraordinary. Behind the supposed pornographer of popular legend lurked the complex mind of an Irish Catholic.

A great artist alters our way of seeing the world. Joyce has permanently altered our view of Dublin, again by making the ordinary extraordinary. Of course, the numerous tourists who come to Dublin to do the rounds of city pubs and streets on 'Bloomsday', 16 June, are seeking a physical Dublin that no longer exists. In two generations much of the fabric of the city has changed beyond recognition. There is now a very expensive city hotel near the Stock Exchange called Bloom's: the hard-pressed advertising canvasser

whom Joyce made the hero of *Ulysses* would have
[2] been astonished. His lunch cost him 7d; today it would
cost him nearly £7. A poor man for most of his life,
Joyce too would have been astonished. Having rejected
him while he was alive, Dublin now finds it can turn a
pretty profit from his posthumous reputation.

Joyce's Dublin has almost disappeared under the
new pressures for redevelopment. But the cityscape
which he created, notably in *Ulysses,* has such a strong
vitality that it imposes itself on the imagination in
its own peculiar way. The types he created in his
books still walk the city streets. The moral dimen-
sions of his art are still valid.

For Joyce himself the city of Dublin and its people
were an obsession. The Irish judge and novelist,
Kenneth Reddin, recalled that during a visit to Joyce
with the painter Patrick Tuohy in the 1930s, the
exile was able to 'name the shops from Amiens Street
to the Pillar. First one side and then the other. When
Tuohy and I left a gap, he filled it. When we named a
new proprietor, he named and remembered the passing of the old.' As Joyce remarked on another occasion to his old college friend C.P. Curran, the lawyer
and architectural historian, why should he return to
Dublin: he had never left it. His memory of the place
was complete. 'Joyce was many things', Curran recalled, 'but he was certainly the last forty volumes of
Thom's Directory thinking aloud.'

James Joyce was, indeed, a man of many parts. This
book, however, is not about Joyce the singer, the
amateur actor, the language teacher, the drinker, the
tweed and fireworks salesman, the lukewarm socialist,
the bank clerk, dog hater, cinema manager, opera lover
or journalist. It is simply about Joyce the writer.

The struggle to write, and then the struggle to get
published, are the main part of every writer's life.
But in Joyce's case his way of life, all those assorted

careers and avocations, and the kind of books he wrote, made for their own peculiar difficulties. He [3] faced these with heroic determination, exemplary fortitude, and other people's money.

Since his death his works and ways have been the object of continuing academic scrutiny, especially in America. The existence of a 'Joyce industry' is notorious. In Ireland it is often lamented. Naturally enough the definitive biography, a large volume running to 842 pages, is the work of an American scholar, Richard Ellmann; though important biographical contributions have been written by several others. Such books, and even less a brief account such as this, can never be a substitute for Joyce's own books.

Only very slowly have Joyce's works made their way against hostility and incomprehension to a wider audience. Their supposed difficulty has stood in the way of even the interest aroused by their obscenity, that is until they became a matter for study at school and university. Yet it was not until the film version of *Ulysses* and the appearance of the books as paperbacks in America and Britain in the 1960s that they became widely read. But even so Joyce will never be a 'popular writer' for reasons which the story of his life will show.

The lives of many writers can be safely separated from their creations. But Joyce's themes of city life, religion, sex, family, revolt and betrayal arise from his own very personal experiences. Though some knowledge of the singer and the cinema manager is essential for a full understanding of Joyce's work, it is the work which makes the life of interest.

* * *

The man himself was a striking figure.

From his youth he carried himself, even in the dark days of adversity, with style. The cheap tennis shoes

which poverty forced him to wear as a student were
[4] set off by the nonchalance of a cane. Later on, when
he could afford to, he dressed with careful elegance.

He was well aware of himself and the effect he made.
Some photographs taken at various times of his life
illustrate this. In 1904 Joyce's friend C. P. Curran
photographed the young poet, aged 22, in the garden
of his parents' house against the background of a glass-
house. Joyce gazes at the camera with a quizzical,
cocky, confident air. Asked what he was thinking
about, he said he was wondering if Curran would ever
lend him five shillings.

In 1939, *Time* Magazine, which was publishing a
long review of *Finnegans Wake,* commissioned the
French photographer Gisèle Freund to make a portrait
of Joyce in colour for the cover of that edition. She
took a long series of pictures, one of which was finally
used. In them Joyce appears aged, ill, and wan, a man
burdened by the troubles of life and the difficulties
of his art. The contrast with the young man of 1904
is complete.

Suffering had marked him. 'For we must never
forget,' John Montague remarks, 'that he had endured
that most heady of agonies, the surgeon's knife on
the optic nerves. The brow is pain creased, the features
lengthen or whiten, but even pain cannot obliterate
that fierce commitment. Sometimes the whole face
seems smouldering, eyeballs scorched, portrait of the
artist as a zealot.'

The poet was commenting on the remarkable images
of Joyce created by the painter Louis le Brocquy, ex-
hibited in several countries some years ago. The pictures were not of the young student, the subject of
Ulysses and *A Portrait,* or of the ageing writer who
created them, but of Joyce as a quasi-mythical figure,
Joyce as an idea, as a literary legend. But paintings,
biographies and critical studies are only evaporations

of the original: the real Joyce is now a shelf of eight books, their sizes, dates and places of creation reveal- [5] ing in themselves the story of Joyce's life, Dublin 1882 – Zurich 1941.

1
Childhood and Youth

James Augustine Joyce was born in Dublin on 2 February 1882 at 41 Brighton Square, Rathgar. In later life he regarded his birthday as a lucky day in his personal system of superstitions. So much so that he arranged with great difficulty the publication of *Ulysses* and the public revelation of the cryptic title of *Finnegans Wake* to fall upon it. The year too was auspicious, he later found, for de Valera was also born in 1882: a conjunction of lives that Joyce made of cosmic significance in his last book. For Joyce nothing was ever merely trivial.

Brighton Square was then only newly built, one of those charming Victorian suburbs of warm red brick that give the city of Dublin its real character. It was a quiet residential area, where the Joyces had many friends. It was also an area of eminent respectability, far removed from squalor, poverty and the promptings of literature.

Joyce's first memories, those fragmentary recollections which open his novel account of his youth, were not of Brighton Square, however, nor of another house in Castlewood Avenue to which the family moved shortly after his birth, but of a house beside the sea (indeed almost in the sea) at Bray in County Wicklow.

Bray was then being developed after the advent of the railway had made it accessible from Dublin, and was often spoken of as 'the Brighton of Ireland', but the curving bay and headland were more reminiscent of a hot summer afternoon in the south of France. Bray's version of La Promenade des Anglais ran past the Joyce's house, happy with young girls, those 'sea-side girls' that remained in Joyce's memory for many years to surface again in *Ulysses*. Can it be that his curious love of resorts in later life arose from his early memories of Bray?

The house in Martello Terrace was the home he describes in his first novel, and one of those girls, a neighbour's child, Eileen Vance, was the boy's first love. The children went to the same kindergarten and played together all the time. The Vances were Protestants, however, and Mrs. Conway, a dour pietistical relation who lived with the Joyces as a kind of governess, disapproved, and warned the child that he would burn in hell for playing with heretics. She also told him, and it impressed him to the end of his life, that thunder was a sign of God's anger with the world. So quite early in his life Joyce learned to fear religion. He was presented with an old choice, either his love or his faith. A basic theme of his writings begins here, in the confusions of a child's hopes and longings.

It was while living in Bray that the young Joyce first became conscious of himself and of his family. The Joyces were respectable, middle-class Dubliners of nationalist persuasion, who kept several servants as well as maintaining a governess. This social nuance to Joyce's early childhood is important. Joyce was not the type of Irishman that was to become typical of the country after it gained its independence. Indeed, a once-landed Protestant friend of his, trying to put the proper aspect on the matter for me, said that he was almost Anglo-Irish in his manner.

James was the eldest in a family of ten children, all that survived to his mother from thirteen pregnancies. There were six girls and four boys. James was close to his brother Stanislaus (born in December 1885), [8] but his other brothers and sisters blend into a confused background to the vital energies of the two older boys. They were close enough for James to make use of the feelings and experiences of his brother in his creative work. Stanislaus kept a diary for many years, and episodes and phrases from his hand were picked up by James for his stories and novels.

Their father, John Stanislaus Joyce, the model for Simon Dedalus, was from Cork; their mother May Murray from Leitrim: a rural mix which produced typical Dubliners. John Joyce had inherited some money and property, but these were slowly lost, partly by unwise investment in a distillery in Chapelizod that went broke, and partly by sheet waste. John Joyce lived well, and well beyond his means. The birth of each child between 1881 and 1894 was associated with a mortgage on his properties in Cork until there was nothing left. Through his political connections (in the time-honoured way of Irish life) he had worked well for Liberal candidates in Dublin — he obtained a position as a Collector of Rates in Dublin, a job which made him, and his son after him, privy to many of the city's secrets. The gossip of local politics and corporation business provided much of the material for *Ulysses* at a later date. And the genesis of *Finnegans Wake* was in John Joyce's stalwart defence of his collector's bag from a thieving tramp in the Phoenix Park.

The boy's first lessons were from 'Dante' Conway, as she was called in the family. But John Joyce had pretensions. Nothing but the best education in Ireland would suit his clever eldest son. So Joyce began his formal education with the Jesuit fathers at Clongowes Wood College in September 1888. He was six years and seven months; or 'half past six' as he told the Rector when he arrived, a remark that stuck to him as a nickname for some time after.

Joyce was to remain under Jesuit tutelage until the summer of 1902, fourteen long and formative years. Clongowes is where the long opening section of his novel *A Portrait of the Artist as a Young Man* (1916) is laid. That book gives a vivid interior idea of the life of Stephen Dedalus against which the bare biographical account of Joyce's own life can represent only a faded exterior.

His rector at Clongowes was Fr John Conmee, whom he later presents as an important character in *Ulysses* where his benign spirituality is shown in contrast to the sterile pomp of the lord lieutenant. But the Jesuits were more to Joyce than mere personalities.

The small boy learnt some important lessons at Clongowes, not only in contact with his contemporaries, but also from the course of studies laid down by the Jesuit tradition. The rudiments of religion and a humane education -- which were never to leave him -- were absorbed in these years. However, the small boy, 'more delicate than brilliant' a Jesuit father later recalled, made little impression on school life during his three years at the college. At the school he was mixing with the sons of prosperous business men and civil servants, as well as some landlords, the makers of modern Ireland, if not yet its owners. Yet he made and kept no friends from these years.

In the spring of 1891 Joyce fell ill – perhaps as a result of being pushed into the schoolyard privy as he described in his novel – and had to have the attention of a doctor as well as the school matron Nanny Galvin. Though he returned as usual for the autumn term, he was withdrawn for good before Christmas 1891. That year Mr Joyce's position had been abolished, and he received a pension only after special pleading by his distraught wife. The increased financial difficulties of living on £132 a year meant the end of Clongowes, at £25 per annum, music extra. Joyce's

final fees, a sum of £27/10/6, remained unpaid,
[10] though they were optimistically demanded to no avail
in September 1901. But little James owed a debt to
the Jesuits beyond that sum of money. Much later he
praised them for teaching him 'to arrange things in
such a way that they become easy to survey and to
judge'. These powers of intellectual discrimination
were no mean gift. The Jesuit claim that given a boy
at seven he is theirs for life would be borne out in the
future career of the writer.

The easy days by the sea were over for the Joyces,
marked finally by the fateful Christmas of 1891.
There had already been months of crisis over Parnell's
leadership of the Irish party. The great hero of the
nation, who had been a main agent in securing tenant
right for Irish farmers, and so beginning the great
social and political revolution which was to overtake
Ireland in a generation, had been shown to be all too
human. At the end of 1889 Captain William O'Shea
had named Parnell as co-respondent in his divorce
suit against his wife. The decree *nisi* was granted, and
followed in November 1890 by a final decree. Mrs
O'Shea, who had been Parnell's mistress for a decade
and had borne his children, was free to marry him.
At first Parnell stood firm against the storm of
protest. But slowly opinion in the party turned against
him. In December 1890 the party, so long a model of
unity, split.

The political struggle became even more bitter and
personal. John Joyce, and after him his son, supported
Parnell. Then suddenly on 6 October 1891, Parnell
died, leaving the divided nation even more shocked.

In his novel Joyce gives a vivid impression of the
passions which the affair aroused in Ireland, the
political rancour, the anti-clerical bile. His first
'published' work was a poem attacking Tim Healy,
the Nationalist MP who later became governor-general

of Ireland, for betraying Parnell. The poem was called 'Et Tu, Healy'. His father was so impressed with this [11] juvenile effort that he had it printed up and distributed it to his friends. He even claimed to have sent a copy to the pope. But no copy is now known to survive, and this little yellow broadsheet remains to be discovered still, the rarest item in the Joyce bibliography.

By contrast Joyce was also writing a great deal of religious poetry at this time, which impressed his mother even more. But none of this survives either.

The fall of Parnell came at the same time as the fall of the Joyces, and the national and personal disasters remained linked forever in Joyce's imagination. The family moved away from Bray to a house in Carysfort Avenue in Blackrock, called Leoville because of the heraldic lion crouching over the front porch. The house was distinquished by stained glass panels in the hall door celebrating the love of Dante and Beatrice. These panels may well have inspired Joyce's interest in and lifelong devotion to the Italian poet. The love of Dante for Beatrice became for Joyce a model of a certain kind of poetic love, the love he felt for Eileen Vance now left behind in Bray and for other pale featured girls he met at parties.

Carysfort Avenue was still a respectable address in a good neighbourhood, with a fine park nearby where the boy could run under the direction of his greatuncle. But then suddenly this house was given up, and the family moved across the river Liffey to the north side of the city, into the first and finest of everworsening lodgings.

Even today the river Liffey forms a cultural divide. For Joyce the south side of the city represented childhood, happiness, elegance, calmness and comfort. Here was his university and the National Library. Across the river on the north side were his now sordid homes, and the stews and brothels of [12] poorer Dublin, and the infernal sermons of his Jesuit teachers at Belvedere. With its wretched inhabitants the city might almost have been an illustration of the system of Dante's hell. While his soul was in love with the idea of a pretty girl from the Rathgar area, his body lost its virginity to a young whore on the north side by the bank of the Royal Canal. For Joyce the geography of Dublin was a paradigm of reality.

After their removal to the north side, James and Stanislaus spent a couple of terms with the Christian Brothers at the O'Connell's Schools in North Richmond Street, before returning to the tutelage of the Jesuits at Belvedere College early in April 1893. This short sojourn with the Brothers who had done so much to educate the majority of Irishmen was never referred to by the Joyce brothers. They shared the low opinion of the Brothers expressed so forcibly by their father: 'Paddy Stink and Micky Mud'. Nor was it reported to his first biographer Herbert Gorman, among many other facts which Joyce wished suppressed.

Belvedere was different. Here Joyce was still under the influence of the Jesuits, but he was free in the afternoons and evenings for his explorations of litera-ture and of the city streets. Both were a wonderful education for a growing boy. In *Portrait* the indivi-dual masters at the school are undefined. The changing character of Stephen Dedalus comes to dominate the action and feeling of the book. But at school what Joyce learned was to be of great importance to him. The methods of learning, with their emphasis on classi-cal form and the training of the memory, were later to be of great service to the writer. Though the Jesuits had made some changes in their traditional system to accommodate the needs of the department of educa-tion, their ideal was still to turn out an educated Christian gentleman.

It was at Belvedere that he read, for a state examination, Charles Lamb's *Adventures of Ulysses,* a book [13] which charmed and enchanted him at once. Outside the school he was reading his way through the English novelists who might be borrowed from Capel Street public library, such as Dickens, Thackeray and George Eliot. Even Thomas Hardy, though there was some concern over *Jude the Obscure.* The librarian mentioned this title to John Joyce. Aroused, he sent Stanislaus along to the library to obtain a copy for him to look through. But in his confusion the boy asked for *Jude the Obscene.*

Joyce was a good and diligent student, but over the years his talents showed a marked preference for languages over mathematics and science. He did well enough in his examinations, however, to gain government scholarships for several years running, money which made a great difference to his family in their now straitened circumstances.

There is little doubt that his teachers, in view of his intelligence and his obvious religious bent, seriously considered him as a possible future member of the Society of Jesus.

Religion, absorbed through his mother's influence on the growing boy, had marked Joyce's life. He had always been a devout schoolboy: that he failed to remain a devout adult was due largely to the personal problems of his late teens. We know, for instance, that he was a leading member of the Sodality of the Blessed Virgin, and that he took his duties in that role with appropriate seriousness. But he was moving into his teens, and his troubled emotions sought for an outlet.

As he describes almost too convincingly in his novel, the cheap vices of the city streets came easily and early to those who sought them: he claimed to have had that first whore when he was only fourteen.

But after his fall into sin, he swung back into periods of great religious fervour, serving two terms as Prefect of the Sodality, which he could not have done in good conscience if he had been in a state of sin. If his superiors saw in him a future priest, Joyce himself was not unattracted by the idea. Newman, after all, was both priest and writer: both vocations might be possible together.

It was not until he went on to university in 1898 that Joyce really fell away from the practice of his religion, according to Kevin Sullivan whose account of this side of Joyce is more convincing than that in the larger biography by Richard Ellmann. But the Catholic faith and the medieval modes of thought in which he had been trained gave the mind of the mature writer its distinctive caste. His works are saturated with Catholic feeling, albeit alongside material of a less worthy kind. There is a very real sense in which Joyce was a Catholic writer, for his aesthetic looked back to Aquinas and to Aristotle for its authority. It comes as no surprise to learn that Ireland was one of the countries that never banned *Ulysses,* and that the *Osservatore Romano* was able to admire *Finnegans Wake* as a work of the spirit, and to praise the positive qualities of Joyce's writings when he died.

In his last years at school Joyce had begun writing both prose and verse. One of his first efforts was a melodramatic story which he intended to sell to *Titbits*, something he never did, reserving the ambition for Mr Bloom in *Ulysses.* He then began to write a series of prose sketches which he called *Silhouettes,* which combined (if we can judge them from what Stanislaus recalls of them) a maudlin theme with a certain amount of real observation. The poems were collected under the title *Moods,* in which the *fin de siècle* ambience of the period must have been great, perhaps under the influence of Yeats. Nothing sur-

vives of this early work, aside from a polished translation of Horace's ode 'O fons Bandusiae'. However [15]
unremarkable this work may have been it was an indication of the drift of Joyce's ambitions.

More important for his development as a writer
than anything he wrote were the experiences he lived
through. The sudden social descent of the Joyce family
was one traumatic experience. Another was the fearful poverty of the parts of Dublin in which they were
now forced to live. The atmosphere of the stories in
Dubliners as well as many of the characters and situations belong to these years. In ten years the Joyces
passed through eleven houses: unpaid rent causing an
annual upheaval, and another hegira with goods and
chattels, including the family portraits which John
Joyce trailed along with him to the end. For a child
of Joyce's sensitivity the experiences were unpleasant:
the resulting stories were also unpleasant. Joyce the
writer dwelt on the unpleasant because Joyce the child
had dwelt among the unpleasant. The only way in
which something might be rescued from the wreck
was through the art of writing: so it came to seem to
Joyce.

He heard the spiritual call to his real vocation on
the beach of the North Bull in the summer of 1898,
between school and college. His mind and soul were
a mass of doubts and hopes, much as any person's
are at that uncertain age. While wandering along the
shore he came upon a young girl, her skirts gathered
up, gazing out to sea. It was a moment of revelation.
His soul, as he describes in a celebrated passage in
A Portrait, was moved with a feeling of profane joy
which his mind could scarcely cope with, 'crying to
greet the advent of life that cried to him'.

> Her image had passed into his soul for ever and no
> word had broken the holy silence of his ecstacy.
> Her eyes had called him and his soul had leaped to

[16] the call. To live, to err, to fall, to triumph, to re-create life out of life! A wild angel had appeared to him, the angel of mortal youth and beauty, an envoy from the fair courts of life, to throw open before him in an instant of ecstasy the gates of all the ways of error and glory. On and on and on!

2

Student Days

It was at University College in Dublin that James Joyce the clever schoolboy began to develop into James Joyce the precocious artist.

Joyce entered the university, which was also in the charge of the Jesuits, in the autumn of 1898 with great hopes for his future. But it was soon clear to him that if he was to gain a proper education he would have to do it for himself. The college was a curious place. It had its origins in a foundation established by John Henry Newman, whom Joyce admired for the quality of his silver-veined prose. It was also the college where the unfortunate Gerard Manley Hopkins (then unknown as a poet) had dragged out his final years. Hopkins had not thought much of the students he had to teach: Joyce failed to admire the teachers as well.

But the institution in No. 86 St Stephen's Green was then passing through a golden period, not so much in the classroom (for academically the university was indeed limited), but in the generation of talented men who crowded into the meetings of the college societies. From the beginning Joyce stood out.

Con Curran has given us a vivid vignette of how Joyce struck his contemporaries. On the first day of term during the opening English lecture, the professor (Fr Joseph Darlington) asked the assembled students if they had read Stephen Phillips's new play *Paola and*

Francesca. None had, but he added almost at once,
[18] 'Have you read it, Mr Joyce?' Rumours of the clever
schoolboy had drifted over from Belvedere. A bored
voice replied indifferently from behind Curran: 'Yes'.

In the next few years the tall, spare frame of the
poet was to become familiar in the college halls,
though often absent from the college classrooms.
The staff were competent, but little more. Another
professor of English in Joyce's time, Fr George
O'Neill, was a partisan of the Baconian authorship
of Shakespeare's plays. Joyce's language teachers, Fr
Charles Ghezzi for Italian and Édouard Cadic for
French, were native speakers and more talented.
Bored and indifferent Joyce may have been with the
lectures of his teachers, but privately he was familiar
with a wide range of European literature, from Dante
(whom he valued above Milton) to Ibsen (a modern
author whose themes outraged so many people at
that time). Even that play of Phillips may not have
been the only one he read: was he also familiar with
a later one called *Ulysses?*

In Joyce's contempt for the college, and beyond it
the city of Dublin, during this period it would be as
well to see a large dose of juvenile bile. The reality
appeared to less partisan witnesses, such as Curran
and Padraic Colum and his wife Mary, to be somewhat
different.

Many of those contemporaries whom Joyce affected
to despise were men of substance who later made
their own mark on the Ireland of their time, both in
life and literature — as did Curran and Colum. Among
those at college with Joyce were men like George
Clancy, future martyred mayor of Limerick; Francis
Skeffington, the radical reformer and pacifist; and
Thomas Kettle, the poet and economist who was
killed in the Great War: men now more admired
in some circles than even Joyce himself.

Indeed, in the matter of contempt, Joyce was somewhat looked down upon by some at the college [19] because he was doing modern languages, 'the girls' course' as his fellow students called it.

Yet Joyce had close friends in college. One, strangely enough, was George Clancy, a straightforward country man who seems to have appealed to Joyce by the very fact of being uncomplicated. He is Davin in *A Portrait*. Another friend with a rural background was J. F. Byrne, from Wicklow. He, however, had a peculiar turn of mind, philosophical and cranky, as his own memoirs reveal. He is Cranly in the novel.

Other close friends were Con Curran, a man of lasting staunchness to Joyce in later years who also helped the student in earlier ones, and Vincent Cosgrave, something of a perennial student through laziness rather than lack of intelligence. In Joyce's life he was to play a sinister role to counter that of Curran.

In the college Joyce soon became one of the well-known characters. He was, as the Dublin expression has it, 'a bit of an artist'. His irreligion and unwashed neck were notorious. But Joyce's interests were of a serious nature, and unaffected by a few lice in his hair. In 1899 he refused to sign a student protest against Yeats's new play *The Countess Cathleen,* which some pious Catholics in the city considered blasphemous (though Yeats had the theological opinion of a distinguished Jesuit that it was not). Joyce was not the only student who declined to sign; indeed out of the whole college only thirty-three students put their names to the petition. The play was an early product of the National Theatre Company, part of the Irish Revival which Yeats was busy directing and encouraging; the protest was a manifestation of the new wave of nationalism that was beginning to roll across the country. Joyce was

enthralled neither by the Revival nor by its opponents.
[20] He was intent on making his own way.

He did, however, become involved with the Gaelic League for a short time, attending lessons in Irish. One of his teachers was Patrick Pearse, for whom he did not much care. In his novel and in the unfinished draft *Stephen Hero,* Stephen Dedalus does the same because he wishes to cultivate the friendship of a girl. In real life the same reason may have held. Yet Joyce's interest in the language may also have been serious: in 1901 both he and Stanislaus officially admitted on the family census form to a knowledge of Irish, and a great deal of Gaelic surfaces in the text of *Finnegans Wake.*

Though disdainful of the interests of the Irish Revival, Joyce was beginning to make his own literary mark. His close friends, such as George Clancy, Vincent Cosgrave and J. F. Byrne, with whom he discussed his ideas and feelings at length, recognised his special qualities of mind, and expected him to soon reveal them fully. He did not disappoint them.

In March 1900 Joyce read a paper on 'Drama and Life' to the Literary and Historical Society (the L&H) the college debating forum. His piece was by way of being a rejoinder to an earlier paper, but it foreshadows some of Joyce's own later literary ideals. He ended with a plea for real life on the stage, but real life seen with a symbolic shape. This profound study, by the usual standards of college debates, made a deep impression of his abilities on his college contemporaries.

Soon after this came another coup, when he appeared in print, publishing an appreciation of *When We Dead Awaken,* 'Ibsen's New Drama', for which he received twelve guineas from the prestigious *Fortnightly Review* in April 1900. This was his real literary debut, for we can safely discount the juvenile 'Et Tu, Healy'.

And very self-assured it was too, drawing the commendation of the ageing dramatist himself and contact with William Archer, the critic and translator of Ibsen. Joyce's espousal of Ibsen, and other modern continental writers, went quite contrary to the literary trends around him in Dublin. He was already edging towards his own approach to the drama and the novel.

With the money he had been paid, less a little given to his mother for housekeeping, he and his father took a short trip to London, where he was able to meet Archer in person. He and his father spent that summer in Mullingar where his father was sorting out the election lists. There Joyce walked and read, and wrote a play called, perhaps typically, *A Brilliant Career*. This was rather magnificently dedicated to 'My Own Soul'. He sent it to Archer, who provided a puzzled critique, for the play was hopeless as a drama, but yet displayed obvious signs of talent. Joyce destroyed the manuscript.

He was also writing poems at this period, but these were not as significant as the short prose pieces, almost the verbal equivalent the snapshots (then so popular) which he called *epiphanies,* because in them some aspect of life was *shown forth*. But drama still caught his ambitions. He wrote to Ibsen on his seventieth birthday, hinting after his felicitations and homage at the talents of a new generation. He was also reading Hauptmann in German, yet another expansion of his horizons.

That year, 1901, he was forced into print again, when an essay he had written was banned from the college magazine, *St Stephen's*. His friend Francis Skeffington had suffered a similar refusal, so they clubbed together to have their papers printed as a pamphlet (for a cost of ten guineas — giving Joyce a taste for this form of semi-private publication, for he resorted to it several times in later life). Skeffington was typically concerned with a topic of public concern, [22] the place of women in the university. So was Joyce's contribution also of public interest, for it was called 'The Day of the Rabblement' and was an attack on the Irish literary movement under Yeats for pandering to popular taste rather than leading it on to better things — such as modern continental dramatists.

However, a paper he read to the L&H in 1902 on James Clarence Mangan, the perennially neglected Irish poet, was published in *St Stephen's*. Here Joyce was more in tune with the tastes of his fellows. But it was the pervasive melancholia of Mangan that appealed to him, rather than the poet's colourful ideas about the Irish past.

It was during these years at college that Joyce finally lost his faith, not as a consequence of one grand gesture of revolt, but by a slow process of attrition which had been going on since his teens. At school he had been a faithful, indeed diligent Catholic, save for short lapses. But then he had been under the active religious guidance of the Jesuits. University College, much to the regret of the Jesuits, made no provision for a course of religious or philosophical instruction at that level. The students were left to face the educated world with what they had taken in at school, and received no complete intellectual view of their religion such as Catholic university graduates might be expected to have.

Nothing in the way of religion was provided which might have the caught the attention of a mind like Joyce's and held his intellectual allegiance. As his interests in literature expanded, his religious life narrowed. Though he seems to have taken a slight part in the Sodality and in the Thomas Aquinas Society, he soon left them. Yet to the end of his life he maintained a relationship of a kind with the Catholic faith: when he thought his wife in danger of death, he even resorted to prayer. But this act of hope in a moment of personal crisis was not typical. If he attended a religious service, as he often did in later years, he did so out of an aesthetic interest in the ceremonies. Asked later in life if he had found something to replace religion, he replied, 'Madam, I said I had lost my faith, not that I had lost my mind'. Religion was something irrational, but like all artists Joyce was fascinated by the irrational.

Joyce's separation from the Catholic Church has to be seen in the context of the ever worsening conditions at home. His father had long since given up any pretence of seeking new employment. On the small sums of money he gave her, May Joyce struggled to keep the family going. Life had become uncomfortable and sordid, a mere existance, the nadir of which was the death of his young brother George of typhus in 1902.

Joyce was sensitively conscious of the gap between the home life of so many of his friends and the conditions which his once comfortable family now endured. He has been accused of snobbery by some critics, but the desire to cast off poverty cannot be classed as that. He put a brave face on affairs: asked what his father's occupation was, he answered, 'Going in for competitions'.

In June 1902 Joyce graduated from university, passing without making any real attempt to excel and taking his degree in Modern Languages. He was by now not only fluent in English, Irish and Latin, but also in French, Italian and German. He had also acquired some literary Norwegian, which he had learned in order to read Ibsen in the original. A choice of career now became a problem. The Jesuits offered him a minor teaching post at the college, but he refused this. His brother later admitted this was a foolish act. Their father urged him to take up a

clerkship at Guinness's brewery, for that at least
[24] would have a good pension — a point of paramount
importance to Irish parents of that and later generations. But pensions had small appeal when the job
itself would be stiffling.

Money was a prime consideration. He decided that
a medical degree would be an advantage. Doctors
were always needed: the hero of his play had been a
doctor. His literary work could easily be continued
on the side, as his ideas only matured slowly. He
registered as a student at St Cecilia's Medical School,
an adjunct to the university, and began there in
October 1902.

He did not stay long, for at the same time he was
making contacts in the small literary world of Dublin.
He began by seeking out George Russell, the mystic
poet who was also the influential editor of the
Irish Homestead, the newspaper of the Co-Operative
Movement. Russell was deeply involved with the
Dublin Theosophical movement as well, and Joyce
was interested in some of the ideas of esoteric Budd-
hism, such as the cycles of history and reincarnation.

Calling on Russell at home one August evening in
1902, Joyce wished to talk about literature. But as
Russell found the young man had a low opinion of
everyone else, and was even diffident about Joyce's
own poems which Russell felt showed some merit.
Later Russell recalled that he told Joyce that 'You
have not enough chaos in you to make a world',
a strange verdict in retrospect.

From Russell, Joyce was passed on to Yeats and
to Lady Gregory. Yeats was in a position to introduce
Joyce to editors, which he did; and Lady Gregory
might be able to assist the young poet with money.
Even at this date Joyce made a deep impression on
these writers. George Moore, then living in Dublin,
had even read 'The Day of the Rabblement' which

was he thought 'preposterously clever', little realising that a rival to his standing as a novelist was emerging. [25] Meeting Yeats, Joyce was out to set him right about nearly everything that the poet had worked for. On leaving, Joyce said he was twenty and asked how old was Yeats. Yeats told him, deducting a year. Joyce sighed. 'I thought as much. I have met you too late. You are too old.' Yeats was slightly shaken by this interview, realising that a younger generation was already knocking at the door.

The ever practical Lady Gregory asked him out to dinner, an unusual event in the young student's life.

In the autumn of 1902 Joyce began his medical studies, but he found he did not care for the scientific aspects of the course. He would, it seems, have liked to obtain a doctor's fees without the trouble of a doctor's education. On 31 October he took his degree, amid a silly demonstration on the part of the students involved, Joyce making a speech defending their right to make as much noise as they liked. This juvenile behaviour was indicative of his unsettled state of mind; in a few weeks he was bored of medicine.

At this moment the family was also in upheaval. John Joyce had even less money to devote to his eldest son's academic endeavours. He had purchased a house (7 St Peter's Terrace, Phibsborough) by cutting his pension in half, leaving him with little more than £5 a month to support the family, none of whom were making any headway with supporting themselves.

To escape from his family and from Dublin, Joyce decided he would go to Paris and continue his medical studies there. He wrote to the authorities in Paris, and began his preparations. The whole scheme was probably a mistake, as his French was not up to the standard that would be required for scientific studies. Lady Gregory, approached for a loan, suggested that he be sure to take warm clothing with him. But [26] she did get him an introduction to the editor of the Dublin *Daily Express* who agreed to take him on as a reviewer. Yeats also agreed that he would see what could be done in London if Joyce visited him there on his way to France. This he did, and though nothing much came of the London introductions, in the course of the next year Joyce was to publish twenty-seven reviews in the *Daily Express*.

Joyce left Dublin on 1 December 1902. He spent a day in London with Yeats, through whom he met Arthur Symons, a meeting which elated him. His new adventure augered well. In Paris he stayed in the Hotel Corneille, a haunt of impecunious Anglo-Saxon students of all kinds. He looked up some people to whom he had introductions. These included Maud Gonne, but finding her and her daughter immured by quarantine, never pursued the matter.

His hopes of a medical course were frustrated first by the problem of gaining a late admission to the courses, and that obtained, by the discovery that he would have to pay for them at once. Furthermore, the level of French was beyond him. Soon he was reporting in his letters home symptoms of ill health that alarmed his mother. So even though he had managed to obtain a pupil for private language lessons, he was happy enough when his parents (by means of yet another mortgage) sent him the money for his fare home. Passing through London once again, he arrived in Dublin on 23 December. The great adventure had come to a swift and shabby end.

A slightly risqué postcard which he had sent to Cosgrave was the cause of a falling out between Joyce and his friend Byrne. This friendship had been important to Joyce, as we can see in its fictional counterpart in *A Portrait*, and he attempted to mend the breach. Byrne, however, would not be fully reconciled: there were elements of Joyce's character, that delight in the sordid which also comes out in his novels, which Byrne could not accept.

But Joyce made other contacts, especially at the National Library. There he met another young poet, Oliver St John Gogarty, a medical student also, who might replace Byrne very well. But soon he was off to Paris again, not to continue with his medical career, but to gain experience of real life. So he continued for some months, living a raffish and often hungry life in Paris. He met John Synge there, and read some of his unpublished writings, which did not impress him. Joyce was not yet at a stage to be impressed by anyone.

He was also writing, a couple of poems, some fifteen epiphanies, and had plans, as he told his mother in a letter, for a play, a book of verses, and an 'Esthetic', all to be published over the following fifteen years. Surviving on small sums of money sent with great hardship from home, he entered into the café life of the city. He even managed some trips outside it. But his life of leisurely poverty was interrupted by a stark telegram at Easter: 'MOTHER DYING COME HOME FATHER.'

He left Paris on 11 April. His mother, he knew, had been complaining of her health for some time and he arrived in Dublin to find the situation was quite as serious as his father claimed. May Joyce *was* dying. Her son was deeply affected by her last, long, lingering illness. She was suffering agonies from what her doctor thought was cirrhosis of the liver, but was in fact cancer. James put this down to the life of appalling hardship which his father's improvidence had brought upon her since 1891. She had not been reared for poverty, and neither had her children. They lacked the essential arts of survival although they would soon have to learn them.

His love for his mother, which was deeply rooted [28] in his childhood, became concentrated into the last months of her life, as did his dislike of his father. In his youth John Joyce had suffered from syphilis (as he admitted when an old man to Dr J. J. Walsh), and as his death certificate puts it, he died of 'senile decay', probably a euphemism for the tertiary stage of the disease. His son (as *Ulysses* and *Finnegans Wake* seem to suggest) knew this and connected it in his mind with the ruin of his family, his mother's death, perhaps his own failing eyesight. (There is no evidence that Joyce himself ever contracted syphilis, though at several times in his life he did have other venereal complaints.) Joyce became determined to break with his family, as he had already broken with the Catholic Church.

He distressed his family by refusing a brusque request from a relative to kneel in prayer by his mother's bedside. But she was already in a coma and would not have benefited from this gesture, which would have gone against his own conscience. There was no going back on such a public 'non serviam'.

In August 1903 his mother died and Joyce had passed an important landmark in his life. He must somehow strive for a new beginning. This he would be able to do only by breaking with his country as well as with his religion and family.

3

Going into Exile

In the fateful months after his return from Paris in
April 1903 to see his dying mother Joyce did little
enough with himself, except hang around the streets
of Dublin. At the time it seemed a useless existence
to his family and friends. Nevertheless the events of
these months were to be of great importance to him,
both in providing the impetus to write and the
materials worked into the fabric of *Ulysses* a decade
later.

These months saw the publication of his first stories,
an initial step in his real career. But for the most part
he read and wrote, saw his friends and enemies, and
drank. As he had little to eat during these months
— for he had almost no money — what he did drink
was almost lethal in its effect. This unhappy period
established a pattern of alcoholism that was to
slowly undermine his health, perhaps even in the end
contributing to his death.

His reading was done, as usual, in the National
Library. His mother's death had a profound effect on
Joyce, perhaps deeper than has been realised. Among
the books he pored over, one of the librarians later
recalled, was the recently published work by the
eminent British psychist F. H. Myers, *Human Personality and Its Survival After Bodily Death,* which was
received in October 1903 according to the stamp on
the Library copy. What strange consolations, emotional
or intellectual, was he drawing from that curious

work in the unhappy winter of 1903? He had long [30] rejected the orthodox doctrines of the Church on this topic: art, however, might provide his own personality with a different kind of survival. The ghost that haunts Stephen in *Ulysses*, the revanent of his tormented mother, had her origin here.

Joyce at the time was having nightmares in which skulls and bloody heads appeared. These he later transferred to Stephen. When the ghost appears to him in the brothel scene in *Ulysses*, Stephen appeals to it for 'the word known to all men', the secret of the dead. But there is no direct answer from the dead, only a mother's memory of her love and pity for her child. If anything did survive of human personality, *Ulysses* suggests, it was love and pity. These were emotions Joyce came to know at this time.

Despite his appearance of going to the dogs, Joyce was in fact preparing himself for his work. For he was also writing. His most important literary effort was a long essay narrative begun on 7 January 1904, which he hoped to place in a new magazine run by two friends called *Dana,* entitled 'A Portrait of the Artist'. This piece was exactly what it claimed to be, a portrait of the writer himself. But the editors, disturbed by his sexual frankness, rejected the essay, declining to print what they considered to be both unreadable and too intimate. The revelations of the young writer's private life, though discreetly described, were a little too much for staider spirits than James Joyce.

At once Joyce began to draft a novel along the same thematic lines. It was planned on a grand scale, a thousand pages at least, and he worked on it with great concentration and speed in the first months of the year. Soon close friends such as Cosgrave and Curran were reading chapters as they were completed.

The novel was called, after a suggestion by Stanislaus Joyce, *Stephen Hero,* and charted the artist's growth from childhood on. Though it was to be left unfinished and was put aside after some 600 pages had been written, it contained the genesis of *A Portrait of the Artist as a Young Man* and *Ulysses.* So from a few brief pages scribbled down in a day Joyce drew out a lifetime's work.

At this time he was also placing poems in *Dana* and other literary journals such as the *Speaker, Saturday Review,* and *The Venture.* George Russell asked him for some short stories for the paper he edited for the co-operative movement, the *Irish Homestead.* As he was to be paid for these at a pound a piece Joyce obliged, and sent in the first versions of 'The Sisters', 'Eveline' and 'After the Race', stories which were later to form part of *Dubliners.*

Here he found a use for the small prose pieces he had been collecting for some time which he called 'epiphanies'. These early versions were very different in tone and texture from the final versions which he published in 1914. For instance, in the volume version of 'The Sisters' there is a reference to the 'Freeman's General', which many readers must have supposed was a misprint carried over from edition to edition. But in the first version of the story we are told that this was how one of the sisters always pronounced the name of the leading Dublin daily, the *Freeman's Journal.* Joyce later kept in the detail, but cut out his original explanation of it.

This method of building up the details of his fictions, often from personal sources, but leaving his readers in the dark as to the full significance of their meaning or *raison d'etre,* was one which Joyce was slowly to develop throughout the rest of his career. In 'the Freeman's General' we can detect the beginnings of that word-play which was to overwhelm the narrative of *Finnegans Wake.*

Joyce was eventually paid for these stories, but money was so short that he had to turn his mind to other schemes for making a living. He was a talented singer. Encouraged by the example of John McCormack whom he met at this time, Joyce raised the fee to enter the Feis Ceoil (the local music competition), which had been the starting point of McCormack's fame. He took singing lessons to improve his voice, and requiring a piano to practise with, he seized the opportunity to move across the city to a room in Ballsbridge which he fitted up with an instrument obtained on credit.

After a couple of concert appearances, he sang at the Feis on 16 May 1904. After two set pieces he was given a simple piece to sing at sight. Joyce waved it away and left the platform. The judge, who had planned to give him the gold medal, was astonished. When another singer was disqualified, Joyce obtained the bronze instead. But unlike the gold medal he might have had if he had been less hasty (for he must have known that he would have to sing on sight), it had no value in a pawnshop. He threw it into the Liffey, but kept the press cuttings which might have some future value. Though one of his teachers offered to train him free for three years, Joyce refused. The stern life of a professional singer did not appeal to him.

Instead he took a temporary position as a teacher in a Dalkey preparatory school, but teaching the dull-minded sons of the genteel required another kind of discipline which he did not have. The episode did, however, provide a setting for the second episode of *Ulysses*. Henceforth, little experience was to be wasted; indeed new experiences were to be sought as material for his work.

His friendship with Oliver Gogarty, then finishing at Oxford, developed. Gogarty proposed that the pair should take quarters together somewhere so that Joyce would have peace to write his novel and Gogarty [33] his poetry. Gogarty took out a lease from the War Office on the old Martello Tower at Sandycove, a sturdy relic of the Napoleonic wars. He went to live there with another friend, named Trench, during the summer. But Joyce delayed until he had to leave his room and could find nowhere else to go without returning to his father's house. It was not until September that he took up residence in the tower, though for *Ulysses* he moved his arrival back some months.

But that was not the only change he made in translating life into literature. The most important event of that summer for Joyce finds no place at all in his novel. For his meeting on 10 June with his wife is omitted completely.

This event was something more than an experience. They met casually on Nassau Street, near the hotel where the girl worked. Her name was Nora Barnacle. She was tall and sturdy with beautiful auburn hair. They made a date which she failed to keep. He arranged another. So on the 16 June 1904 Joyce and Nora walked out together for the first time.

This was an encounter that was to alter his whole life. The young man in a yachting cap and tennis shoes who met Miss Barnacle on that Dublin day in June was searching not only for a way forward in his artistic ambitions, but also for a solution to his emotional problems, some way of uniting the ideal of his soul with the desires of his body. Rejected by women, scornful of whores, betrayed (so he liked to think) by his friends, he walked his own way.

Now for the first time in his experience Joyce achieved an intimate relationship with a girl who did not expect to be paid. Till then he had known only whores, with whom one had sexual intercourse, or

respectable girls, with whom any sort of relationship
[34] seemed difficult to create. Nora changed all that.
Her open frankness won him over. Not surprisingly
he cherished the memory of that date, later making
it the day on which the action of *Ulysses* is set.

Though sexually intimate from that day, their relationship stopped short of intercourse. Some concession
was made to the decorum of the period, for he remained Mr Joyce for a long time before he became Jim.

Joyce was enchanted by what he discovered in
Nora; what Nora made of her Jim is more difficult
to know, as she does not seem to have been as ready
as he was to put her intimate feelings down on paper.
She was, he found, gay and witty; the things she said
so thoughtlessly delighted him. She thought highly
of herself. Yet she had none of that stifling refinement
that smothered the personalities of the more respectable girls he had known at college and earlier. There
was nothing at all contrived or artificial about her and
he liked that. She came into his life so easily, with a
light and confident step. She knew about men well
enough, but her initiative on that first night overwhelmed him. She changed his life so completely in
so short a time that it was easy to be almost in love
with her. But love was a bitter word and he stumbled
over saying it for a long time.

This growing relationship with Nora affected his
friendships. He made it up with Byrne, but not on the
old basis. Cosgrave had left him in the lurch one night
when he got into a fight in St Stephen's Green. With
Gogarty too his relations were under strain. He
planned to find a place for all of these people in his
developing novel. Other events too, such as the night
he was dead drunk in the Camden Hall and had to be
taken home by one of the Fay brothers and another
actor, would be put to good use. But he felt he
needed some kind of climax.

His stay in the tower with Gogarty might serve that purpose, for this experiment came apart with [35] bad feelings on both sides. Gogarty's companion, Trench, was slightly disturbed, and one night awoke in a delerium: thinking he was killing a panther he shot the pots and pans off a shelf over Joyce's bed. Joyce thought Gogarty had encouraged this. He declined to be patronised, and left the next morning at first light. The tower he knew would find a place in his book, but eventually when that book failed, the material broke in two, and the tower provided not an ending for *A Portrait* but a beginning for *Ulysses*.

Joyce was now thinking of going away again. A scheme to play his way with a lute through the south of England seaside towns during the summer came to nothing. The idea of Paris was more tempting. Through the late summer and early autumn there was movement towards departure. Con Curran, who had been reading the chapters of *Stephen Hero,* had remarked on Joyce's 'desperate hunger for truth'. That truth would be better served in exile.

There was nothing now to hold him in Dublin. He had fallen out with Gogarty and with many others, so much so that in July he wrote a satirical broadside, which he later had printed up and distributed to the victims. *The Holy Office* was a strong vituperative piece, almost a casting off of the city and its denizens. His family ties had dissolved with his mother's death. At this time he felt little affection for his father or attachment to his siblings. Involvement with the fate of his brothers and sisters would only prevent him from achieving his full purpose as an artist.

On 13 August the *Irish Homestead* published 'The Sisters'; 'Eveline' followed in September and 'After the Race' in December. But by then the bird had flown. On 2 August he sang at a concert with John McCormack: Nora was delighted. Stories were

all very well, but here was something she understood
[36] and appreciated. Years later she was to surprise
Joyce's rather humourless intellectual friends in
Paris with her sly thought that 'Jim should have stuck
to music instead of bothering with writing'.

After this they seem to have grown closer together.
Some of his feelings can be gained from a letter which
he wrote to Nora two days later, which gives a sharply
pointed pen picture of his life at this time:

I may have pained you tonight by what I said but
surely it is well that you should know my mind on
most things? My mind rejects the whole present
social order and Christianity — home, the recognised
virtues, classes of life, and religious doctrines.
How could I like the idea of home? My home was
simply a middle-class affair ruined by spendthrift
habits which I have inherited. My mother was
slowly killed, I think, by my father's ill-treatment,
by years of trouble, and by my cynical frankness
of conduct. When I looked on her face as she lay
in her coffin — a face grey and wasted with cancer
— I understood that I was looking on the face of a
victim and I cursed the system that made her a
victim. We were seventeen in family. My brothers
and sisters are nothing to me. One brother alone is
capable of understanding me.

Six years ago I left the Catholic Church, hating it
most fervently. I found it impossible for me to
remain in it on account of the impulses of my
nature. I made secret war upon it when I was a
student and declined to accept the positions it
offered me. By doing this I made myself a beggar
but I retained my pride. Now I make open war
upon it by what I write and say and do. I cannot
enter the social order except as a vagabond. I
started to study medicine three times, law once,
music once. A week ago I was arranging to go away

as a travelling actor. I could put no energy into the plan because you kept pulling me by the elbow. The [37] actual difficulties of my life are incredible but I despise them.

When you went in tonight I wandered along towards Grafton Street where I stood for a long time leaning against a lamp-post, smoking. The street was full of a life which I have poured a stream of my youth upon. While I stood there I thought of a few sentences I wrote some years ago when I lived in Paris — these sentences which follow — 'They pass in twos and threes amid the life of the boulevard, walking like people who have leisure in a place lit up for them. They are in the pastry cook's, chattering, crushing little fabrics of pastry, or seated silently at tables by the café door, or descending from carriages with a busy stir of garments soft as the voice of the adulterer. They pass in an air of perfumes. Under the perfumes their bodies have a warm humid smell' —

While I was repeating this to myself I knew that that life was still waiting for me if I chose to enter it. It could not give me perhaps the intoxication it had once given but it was still there and now that I am wiser but more controllable it was safe. It would ask no questions, expect nothing from me but a few moments of my life, leaving the rest free, and would promise me pleasure in return. I thought of all this and without regret I rejected it. It was useless for me; it would not give me what I wanted.

This old life, the one of dissipation he had led in Nighttown with Gogarty and Cosgrave, was behind him. Having rejected what Ireland had to offer there was only one way out. He decided to go to Europe. He easily persuaded Nora to go with him, a chance

she took, so unlike the girl Eveline in his short
[38] story. Eveline resisted at the last moment the promptings of her lover to follow him abroad to a new life
in South America. Nora had no such qualms.

For nothing held Nora either. A provincial girl,
she had no ties in Dublin. She came, in Galway,
from a troubled family. Her father was a baker by
trade, a drunk by choice. He had deserted her mother
and she had been brought up by her grandmother.
After a family row she had left home: one of her
uncles had objected to the company she was keeping.
What Joyce offered her was perhaps more than she
might have expected. She too was rejecting her family,
disdaining the demi-monde into which she might so
easily have fallen.

They had made up their minds by the middle of
September. They decided to go away as soon as
possible. He left her in no doubt about the hazards
of what they were about to do. But she was not
inclined to change her mind.

Joyce bustled about his preparations. He applied
for a teaching post with the Berlitz language schools,
hoping for a job in Paris or in Scandinavia. Finally he
thought he had obtained a position in Trieste, at that
time a city in the Austrian Empire. Paris would have
to wait.

So in October 1904 Joyce and Nora left for
Europe. Though they were to make brief visits in
later years, and though their hearts and minds were
always on their homeland, they were to remain exiles,
vagabonds for the sake of his art, for the rest of their
lives. Going into exile from Ireland, they dispensed
with conventional forms, such as the need to marry.
Nevertheless, they went down to the boat separately,
only meeting aboard, so that their families could not
stop them.

At this moment in his life, the importance of Nora

Barnacle to Joyce should not be underestimated. When his father heard the name of his son's girl, he remarked, [39] 'She'll never leave him'. And she never did. It would be foolish to pretend that the marriage did not have its troubles. Yet through all the tides of their life, all the storms of emotional difficulty and financial trouble, she clung to the rock of his personality. Whether she ever 'understood' him intellectually is doubtful. She had no need to. What she provided him with belonged to some other and far from cerebral part of his life. Nora had restored a precarious balance to his life which had been upset by his mother's death. What he could do with his life remained now to be seen.

Joyce's courage in leaving family and country behind fills one only with a sense of admiration. He seemed, despite his great talents, to have few prospects in Ireland. His friends doubted that a future on the continent with a woman he hardly knew would improve them. By sheer fortitude Joyce overcame all difficulties. But when they sailed from the North Wall on 8 October — Joyce in a pair of black boots borrowed from a friend — the future was dark and their courage all the more remarkable.

Writing years later in exile, Joyce gave expression to this theme of flight in the closing passage of *A Portrait of the Artist as a Young Man,* where his departure for Paris is conflated with his departure with Nora:

April 16. Away! Away!

The spell of arms and voices: the white arms of roads, their promise of close embraces and the black arms of tall ships that stand against the moon, their tale of distant nations. They are held out to say: We are alone — come. And the voices say with them: We are your kinsmen. And the air

[40] is thick with their company as they call to me, their kinsman, making ready to go, shaking the wings of their exultant and terrible youth.

April 26. Mother is putting my new secondhand clothes in order. She prays now, she says, that I may learn in my own life and away from home and friends what the heart is and what it feels. Amen. So be it. Welcome, O life! I go to encounter for the millionth time the reality of experience and to forge in the smithy of my soul the uncreated conscience of my race.

April 27. Old father, old artificer, stand me now and ever in good stead.

With this romantic invocation of the classical figure of his demi-namesake, Daedelus the maker of the labyrinth, Joyce's Stephen Dedalus leaves Ireland. In the manuscript of the novel, now in the National Library of Ireland, the book is dated in Joyce's own hand from homely *Cabra, Dublin 1904* to its eventual completion in alien *Trieste, Austria 1914*. Between those two places lay the labyrinth of the artist's life, the lonely perseverance of the writer with his work, unimagined at departure.

4

Trieste

On their journey by train across Europe Nora began to tell Joyce a little about her life before he met her. These revelations were bound up with the even more emotional experience of being involved permanently with one woman. What he heard of the hardships and frightening experiences of her childhood put his own life into a different perspective. The first hint of Molly Bloom was given him on this journey. Their honeymoon was spent in a small hotel in Zurich and it was there perhaps that Nora told him about Michael Bodkin.

Years before, when she was in her early teens in Galway, she had known, and perhaps even loved a little, a young man some years older than her. He had contracted rheumatic fever, and died young from the weakened heart that resulted. But as she had been forced to give him up a broken heart might have been another reason. It was a touching story, in contrast to some of the other experiences in her life, which seems to have affected Joyce deeply. The idea of the other man in the life of the loyal wife was a paradox which fascinated him from then on. It is a theme that appears in all his writings.

Joyce's intellectual range had always been very great. Now with Nora his emotional horizons began to widen. The student Stephen Dedalus began to give way to the married Leopold Bloom. Nora had brought him, unexpectedly, the greatest gift an artist can gain,

the gift of creative growth, the ability to change into
[42] something new, stronger, more powerful. Nora was the
essential countersign to Joyce's artistic passport.

On 20 October 1904 James and Nora arrived in
Trieste, the main seaport and naval station of the
Austrian Empire on the Adriatic. At that time, though
small enough to know well, Trieste was a busy
cosmopolitan city, filled with Austrians, Italians,
Slavs, Greeks and Jews: all the mingled cultures of
the Mediterranean. The Irish novelist Charles Lever
had been British consul there until 1872, and had been
succeeded by Sir Richard Burton, the infamous
traveller and translator of *The Arabian Nights*. Doubtless Joyce was struck by this conjunction of Irish wit
and humour with sexual scholarship and explicit
candour, as copies of their books were in his library.
They were happy augers for his own literary efforts
in exile.

He began his residence in the Austrian Empire by
getting himself arrested on his first night there, along
with two English sailors with whom he had been
drinking. He was soon released with the aid of the
reluctant British consul, but for the patient Nora
this bibulous spree was only the first of many, that
night the first of many in strange lodgings, abandoned
while Joyce prowled the streets: a situation to which
she would become accustomed in the following years.

It transpired that there had been some confusion
over the job he expected to find waiting for him. The
local Berlitz School knew nothing about him and
said he had been hired by someone with no authority
to do so. But he could not now turn back. For
several days Joyce scrounged around Trieste after
pupils and small loans, both difficult tasks in a city
where he knew nobody.

Then through the good offices of the superior of
the Berlitz School a job was arranged in Pola, an

Austrian naval station fifty miles down the Adriatic coast. The head of the school there met them at the [43] boat — his name was Almidano Artifoni (one later borrowed for a character in *Ulysses*). The young Irish couple were a strange sight, he recalled: Joyce proud and impervious to his circumstances, Nora in a peculiar hat, looking confused and curious. They found a flat in Via Gulia 2, near the Berlitz School, and Nora began her housekeeping among the borrowed pots and pans, troubled by the last lingering mosquitoes of late summer.

They settled into a sort of life, adjusting to each other. Nora found cooking tedious, and as often as not they ate out cheaply. She was pregnant by now, which added to their difficulties. She was also religious which he was not. One night Joyce had a severe cramp in his stomach and Nora prayed, 'O my God, take away Jim's pain'. Jim himself had little faith in prayer. That severe pain would recur over the years, especially at moments of crisis. Was it perhaps the first symptoms of the duodenal ulcer that would eventually flare up with fatal consequences in Zurich in 1941?

At Christmas Nora found the flat unbearable. Pregnancy and the festive season were doubtless making her more wretched than she really was. The deputy head of the school offered them room in his house. They moved there in January 1905. But this was only a temporary arrangement: for they finally returned to Trieste in March.

There they continued to live a restricted life in cheap flats. Nora found this trying, as she spoke only a few words of the local patois, did not understand what Joyce was trying to do with his writing, and felt sick all the time. The baby was born on 27 July. It was a boy and they called it George, after Joyce's dead brother. He telegraphed his family:

SON BORN JIM. To which Vincent Cosgrave added
[44] as the message made its way among his friends:
MOTHER AND BASTARD DOING WELL. John
Joyce, however, who had been shocked by their
ménage, was delighted at the thought of a grandchild.

The baby was not baptised. Joyce had now given
another hostage to fortune. His teaching work brought
in very little money, and was not, in any case, an
occupation with much future in it. It was thought
of as merely a temporary resort, as were the small,
dingy flats in which the couple lived during these
years. But like the flats, the teaching lasted for
decades. Meantime it was important to set about
making his name as a writer.

Work was continuing on the novel he had begun
before leaving Dublin. Chapters would be sent off to
his brother and a few close friends for their comments,
although no end of the work was in sight. But the
collection of short stories was complete. During this
year Joyce submitted to the London publisher Grant
Richards his collection of lyrices, *Chamber Music,*
over which he had laboured for the last couple of
years. Richards turned them down: there was no
market for verse by an unknown poet. This rebuff
did not prevent Joyce, a little later, from submitting
to Richards the collection of stories now entitled
Dubliners. These did interest Richards, and he agreed
to publish them. Joyce was delighted.

But his hopes were premature. The printer to whom
Richards sent the copy declined to print several
passages in the text which he considered too outspoken.
Richards sent the manuscript back to Joyce, who
agreed to make the required changes, much as it
pained him. In June 1906 he wrote to Richards:

It is not my fault that the odour of ashpits and
old weeds and offal hangs around my stories. I
seriously believe that you will retard the course

of civilisation in Ireland by preventing the Irish people from having one good look at themselves [45] in my nicely polished looking-glass.

Joyce had begun his long campaign to have his work published as he had written it. Eventually Richards refused to issue the book at all, having convinced himself that he was leaving his firm open to prosecution for publishing an obscene libel.

The young couple in Trieste, surviving in cramped quarters, were now joined by Stanislaus Joyce, who began to play an even larger role in his brother's life, as his conscience, whetstone and bailer-out.

In his own memoirs, *My Brother's Keeper,* and in the influence he exercised over Richard Ellmann's presentation of Joyce, Stanislaus has presented their earlier life in Dublin from his own peculiar viewpoint. The same relationship was to continue until 1914. Their minds were contrasting though congenial, and this was important to Joyce. Though Nora catered to his emotional and sexual needs, she was limited in her mental outlook. Always Joyce looked for, and found, intellectual stimulation with other men.

In 1906 the family left Stanislaus and moved to Rome, where Joyce obtained a job as a foreign correspondent in a bank. It was not a job that interested him much, nor did he and Nora find Rome as attractive as he had hoped they might. So the following year they were back in Trieste again. Joyce now survived by giving private lessons in English (rather than through a school), and though this did not pay very well it left him free for his literary work.

Stephen Hero, which was to have covered his childhood and university years in some sixty-four chapters running to about a thousand pages, was finally abandoned. Clearly the old-fashioned narrative form which he had chosen was too conventional for what

he really wanted to do. He cannibalised the manuscript
[46] and began to rework it as a new book portentously
called *A Portrait of the Artist as a Young Man,* which
he finally completed in 1914, following the near loss
of the original manuscript when Nora threw it on the
fire after a family row. Here he employed a brilliant
impressionistic technique to cover in a few hundred
pages what had taken ten times as many before. The
trudging realism of the earlier work gave way in the
final novel to a vivid, dream-like, episodic style.

Meanwhile some small progress was made. Joyce's
first published literary work, *Chamber Music,* appeared
in 1907 from Elkin Matthews in London, who had
accepted the work on the advice of Arthur Symons
whom Joyce had met through W. B. Yeats. In this
slim volume he collected together the poems he had
begun writing in his last years at school and first years
at college. They were mannered poems in an Elizabethan style, carefully arranged by mood and meaning.
The general theme of the series was the vagaries of
love. The earlier poems are artificial in their melancholy
but in one or two of the later poems the theme of
betrayal and the hopelessness of love becomes domi-
nant. The volume ends on a low passive note: as in
this poem, much admired by Yeats:

I hear an army charging upon the land
　　And the thunder of horses plunging,
　　　　foam about their knees.
Arrogant, in black armour, behind them
　　　　stand,
　　Disdaining the reins, with fluttering
　　　　whips, the charioteers.

They cry unto the night their battlename:
　　I moan in sleep when I hear afar their
　　　　whirling laughter.
They cleave the gloom of dreams, a blinding
　　　　flame,

Clanging, clanging upon the heart as upon
    an anvil.   [47]

They come shaking in triumph their long
    green hair:
    They come out of the sea and run shouting
    by the shore.
My heart, have you no wisdom thus to
    despair?
    My love, my love, my love, why have you
    left me alone?

At the time the poems earned their author little apart from a place in a few anthologies. But as poems they would now be of little interest were it not for the nature of Joyce's later work. The musical qualities (so obvious above) of the poems appealed, however, to a generation for whom singing held a greater place than now, and some were set to music and were sung, often by Joyce and his son George at parties in Paris in the 1920s.

Joyce now had at last a real book to show for his labours. He was also writing articles on literature and Irish affairs for a Trieste newspaper, *Il Piccolo della Serra*. And in 1907 Nora also gave birth to a daughter on 26 July. The child was born in the poor ward of the local hospital, its parents having no money: literature was not profitable. Joyce himself was taken to the same institution at the time with an attack of iritis. The long and painful siege of his sight had begun. The girl was called Lucia, after the patron saint of light and eyes.

In 1909, in the hope of improving his income, Joyce returned to Ireland, where he hoped to arrange for the publication of his stories with the Dublin firm of Maunsel and Co., who published J. M. Synge and other well known writers of the Irish Revival. Later in the year he was to make a second trip to Dublin.

These visits were to have the most profound consequences both for his writing and his relations with
Nora.

By this date he was coming into his full powers as
a writer. The stories he had assembled from 'The
Sisters', written in 1904, to 'The Dead', written after
his stay in Rome, demonstrated this authority. When
Dubliners finally appeared after the author's long
struggle with various publishers, its impact was muted,
though it was obvious that Joyce's early claims were
not as unfounded as some unfriendly people in
Dublin had thought — or hoped.

These stories formed a moral history of the city
and its people, and many readers who thought the
stories unlovely and the people in them repellent
might have wondered whether this was the bias of
the author or the nature of his native city.

Though the stories had been written over several
years, and their sources varied in time and place,
Joyce carefully arranged them so as to reveal an
ever-widening experience of life.

The book opens in childhood with the juvenile
experience of death, moves on through sexual misadventures of 'An Encounter', 'Araby' and 'Eveline',
towards the maturing experiences of a young man in
'After the Race', 'Two Gallants' and 'The Boarding
House'. Then follow four stories of maturity, of
failed family life in 'A Little Cloud' and 'Counterparts',
of sterile relations in 'Clay' and 'A Painful Case'.
The last four stories move on to deal with social
groups: politics in 'Ivy Day in the Committee Room',
artistic life in 'A Mother' and religion in 'Grace'.

The collection was created with a meticulous eye
for detail. The situations were all derived from personal experience. The earliest related to his own
childhood. He and his brother Stanislaus had been
the two boys who played truant from school and,

wandering through the open fields of Ringsend, had met the 'queer old josser' recreated in 'An Encounter'. [49] The bazaar held in Ballsbridge had been visited by Joyce, whom a school friend later recalled wandering as if he too had lost something precious. Joyce had written up the Gordon Bennett Race which features in 'After the Race'. The atmospere of 'The Boarding House' owed something to Finn's Hotel where Nora had worked, though the setting was on the northside of Joyce's young days.

Exact details in the other stories were also derived from recorded reality. Joyce's intention was documentary and clinical. He wanted to reveal the inhabitants of Dublin to themselves in a way never attempted before (or indeed since). The collection is almost unique in the exactness of its design and the completeness of its vision. Conceived and written as a piece of the whole, each story, though complete in itself, echoes through all the others to provide an overview of a society in stagnation.

The collection closes with 'The Dead', which is almost a short novel, dealing with the mature realisation of what death means — in contrast to the dim appreciation of it finality by the boy in the opening story, 'The Sisters'. Into the narrative Joyce wove many strands of his own and Nora's past lives. The story of the wife's lost childhood love was a direct transcription of the affection which Nora had known for Michael Bodkin.

While they were travelling out to Trieste from Dublin she had told Joyce the story of their brief friendship which ended with Bodkin's death. Joyce, who easily transformed his own life into literature, was now able to absorb his wife's past into his writing. More than that, he was able to fill it with his new understanding of human relationships which had grown up with his marriage. The story, among the most powerful ever written, closes with one of the most famous passages [50] in Irish literature: Gabriel Conroy is brooding over his wife's feelings for Michael Furey.

Generous tears filled Gabriel's eyes. He had never felt like that himself towards any woman, but he knew that such a feeling must be love. The tears gathered more thickly in his eyes and in the partial darkness he imagined he saw the form of a young man standing under a dripping tree. Other forms were near. His soul had approached that region where dwell the vast hosts of the dead. He was conscious of, but could not apprehend, their wayward and flickering existence. His own identity was fading out into a grey impalpable world: the solid world itself, which these dead had one time reared and lived in, was dissolving and dwindling.

A few light taps upon the pane made him turn to the window. It had begun to snow again. He watched sleepily the flakes, silver and dark, falling obliquely against the lamplight. The time had come for him to set out on his journey westward. Yes, the newspapers were right: snow was general all over Ireland. It was falling on every part of the dark central plain, on the treeless hills, falling softly upon the Bog of Allen and, farther westward, softly falling into the dark mutinous Shannon waves. It was falling, too, upon every part of the lonely churchyard on the hill where Michael Furey lay buried. It lay thickly drifted on the crooked crosses and headstones, on the spears of the little gate, on the barren thorns. His soul swooned slowly as he heard the snow falling faintly through the universe and faintly falling, like the descent of their last end, upon all the living and the dead.

5
Crisis

For Joyce, as for Gabriel Conroy, the time had come to set out on a journey westward. He thought of sending his son Giorgio, as they called him in the family, home to Dublin with Stanislaus in the summer of 1909, when the boy would be four years old. He wrote to ask would he be welcome, but by the spring he had decided he would go himself.

This would enable him not only to show off the boy in person, but also to arrange the publication of his stories with the firm of Maunsels in Dublin. He obtained a year's advance payment for language lessons from one of his pupils, and father and son set out for Ireland, with the added intention of going down to Galway to see Nora's people as well.

On 29 July 1909 the Joyces arrived in Dublin. He noticed Gogarty's fat back on the quay but avoided him. Everyone in the family, he reported to Nora, was delighted with Giorgio. He anxiously reported to Trieste the good opinions of various relatives and Dublin denizens about his appearance and health. He was in good form, and even made soundings about a job which would allow the rest of the family to return.

But his main business was to see to the publication of *Dubliners*. To this end he called on Maunsels and talked to George Roberts, the manager, whom he had known since college (and from whom he had borrowed in the past). But he was told he would have to wait for an answer.

He encountered Gogarty, who invited him to his
[52] house in Ely Place. This contrast with his own poor
flat in Trieste must have made Joyce uncomfortable.
He maintained his distance, though Gogarty was
prepared to forget their past differences. He was well
aware that Joyce planned to deal with the expulsion
from the Tower in his novel, and finally exclaimed
that he did not care what Joyce wrote as long as it
was literature. So the meeting passed off pleasantly
enough. (When *Ulysses* did appear Gogarty was not
so benign. 'That Joyce whom I kept in his youth',
he fulminated, 'has written a book you can read on
the toilet walls of Dublin.')

However, on 6 August Joyce had a more fateful
conversation with his other old friend Vincent
Cosgrave. At this time Cosgrave was still a perennial
student, a not quite failed medical man. Cosgrave had a
malicious streak in him. Earlier he had been the cause
of the breach between Byrne and Joyce. Joyce had put
him into *A Portrait* as Lynch, after the infamous mayor
of Galway. Now in return for the unattractive name
and features which Joyce had given him, Cosgrave
thought he would have some fun with Joyce.

Their talk had turned naturally to earlier years.
Back in that long summer of 1904 Cosgrave had
tried to court Nora, who seemed to him just another
skivvy to have some fun with. Now Cosgrave claimed
that on every second night he also had walked out with
Nora, along the same route as she had walked with
Joyce. Joyce was mortified.

Joyce's whole world seemed to be collapsing around
him. The one steady person in his life had now, it
seemed, betrayed him. What he had always feared was
coming to pass. She was no better than the rest of
her race, informers, traitors, deceiving hyprocrites.
In the first hot flush of his unhappy anger he wrote
her an agonised letter of bitter accusation.

What else, he wondered, had they done together, recalling how open she had been with him. He had been completely frank with her about the sins of his past life, but she (so it now seemed) had held back on him.

He put the latter into the post that night. But he did not sleep. Other thoughts assailed him in the early hours of the morning. Was Giorgio even his son? He calculated dates, brooded upon physiological facts, recalled what Nora had told him about a certain Mr Holohan in the hotel who had tried to seduce her. His heated imagination returned again and again to imagining her with another man.

At half past six he got up, and sitting in the cold morning light wrote a second letter. He would return to Trieste as soon as Stanislaus sent the money, and they would arrange then what was best to do.

O, Nora, is there any hope yet of my happiness? Or is my life to be broken? ... If I could forget my books and my children and forget the girl I loved was false to me and remember her only as I saw her with the eyes of boyish love I would go out of life content. How old and miserable I feel!

From Trieste, where Nora had sought the advice of his brother, a douche of common sense came back to him. Meanwhile he had talked over Cosgrave's claim with his other old friend Byrne, who had returned specially from Wicklow to see Joyce. Joyce and he passed a pleasant afternoon talking in the back room of Byrne's house, 7 Eccles Street, while Giorgio played around the apple trees in the back garden with Byrne's dog Boy. Joyce was to borrow this residence for Mr Bloom when he came to write *Ulysses*. Byrne told him that quite frankly he thought Cosgrave's story was 'a blasted lie'. And so Joyce came to think,

believing that Cosgrave and Gogarty had concocted
[54] it between them to try him out.

Reassured, Joyce went about his business. Soon a contract for *Dubliners* was drawn up by Maunsels and signed. Joyce had hoped to obtain a professorship of Italian at the university, but it transpired that the post would only be a lectureship in commercial Italian, and not a full academic position. But bolstered by his small achievement in obtaining a signed contract, he returned to brooding once again upon his relationship with the distant Nora.

He pleaded with her for her love, wrote of his nights being tortured by the thoughts of her, and urged her to write about her feelings for him. He promised her a present which would remind her always of what they had been through. And yet, 'my jealousy is still smouldering in my heart. Your love for me must be fierce and violent to make me forget utterly.'

After reporting on the first night of Shaw's play *The Shewing-Up of Blanco Posnet* for a Trieste newspaper, he fiddled a press pass for the Galway train and went down to see Nora's family. This visit was a great success. He went around the town looking at the places associated with her childhood, gathered family gossip, and the words of some songs. Among these vital fragments were the words of 'The Lass of Aughrim' which had played such an important part in the texture of 'The Dead', in arousing the wife's memories of her lost childhood love.

On his return to Dublin Joyce set about gathering money for his sister Eva's fare to Trieste. He explained to his protesting brother that she would help around the flat with the housekeeping, at which Nora was so deficient, and she would be some sort of company for Nora as well. He also had a necklace made up for Nora. It comprised five ivory pieces on a gold chain with a larger piece on which was inscribed on one side

Love is Unhappy and on the other *When Love is Away*. He sent this to her with a sad *cri de coeur*, [55] 'Save me from the badness of the world and of my own heart'.

Still he lingered on in Dublin until early September, but finally left on the 9th with his son and his sister. Joyce and Nora greeted each other with tremulous excitement. His last letters to her from Dublin had attempted to heal the breach his jealousy had caused, and were full of his impassioned declarations of love. Though he claimed to be offended by coarse words in the talk around him, he still admitted that he wished to kiss her on a secret place. Stanislaus was sniffy as usual about Jim's behaviour — after all it was his money which had supported both Joyce's journey and Joyce's family while he had been away. But a rupture between the brothers on James's arrival in Trieste was prevented by Joyce's almost immediate return to Dublin.

Eva Joyce quickly became entranced by the novelty of motion pictures, which she first saw shortly after she had settled with her brother's family in Trieste. Joyce leapt eagerly on her casual remark that it was strange that a city as large as Dublin had no cinemas, when they were so tremendously popular in Trieste. Italy was at this time a major producer of films. Joyce saw here yet another opportunity to make his elusive fortune. Having raised financial backing from a group of Triestine businessmen, he departed for Dublin to give his native city its first taste of cinematographic entertainment. By 22 October he was back in Dublin.

The immediate prospects of business in Dublin were quite good. Joyce soon acquired a suitable hall and the various licenses needed, staff were hired, publicity arranged. The cinema was called the Volta and was situated in Mary Street, which Padraic Colum thought a little rough for customers from the south side of the city. Joyce had no doubts and was soon off to Belfast and Cork to look for premises in those cities. He enjoyed being a man of business. It was a pleasant change to have large sums of money passing through one's hands. He was given to flashing wads of notes before friends old and new. He wanted them to see that he was not the drifting waster they had once known, but the trusted colleague of successful businessmen. This was a new role for Joyce, one he played with panache for a little while at least.

The Volta opened to favourable reviews on 20 December 1909. Joyce enjoyed the cinema, and it is probable that the film technique influenced him when he came to write *Ulysses*. The intercutting of the action in the episode of the Wandering Rocks (as he called it in his scheme of the novel), where various characters move through the city streets in the same hour, owes somethings to film form. This was little gain from the venture, for after his return to Austria, the Dublin business declined through mismanagement and had to be sold. What Joyce had hoped to gain financially from his association, he lost.

During this second separation he and Nora, now quite reconciled to each other after the traumatic events of August, were exchanging letters of astonishing intimacy, ranging from the lofty heights of devotion to the most fevered of sexually stimulating prose. Nora's side of this correspondence seems not to have survived. Only Joyce's letters were saved and for many years these letters remained unpublished. When the first volume of Joyce's letters was brought out, the editor, Stuart Gilbert, claimed a little disingenuously that few of Nora's letters survived as the couple had never really been separated. In the later volumes edited by Richard Ellmann, letters from Nora were included, but her more personal and intimate ones had vanished. And even then parts of Joyce's letters, and the complete text of two, were suppressed. When at last they were released in 1975 they created something of a sensation. For the letters were in fact pornographic in a very real sense, intended to arouse and partly satisfy the sexual longings of the separated lovers. When the immediate need was assuaged, Joyce would turn to other matters with a casual *Basta per sesera,* enough for this evening.

Parts of the vanished letters from Nora (which would have been in Joyce's own hands) may well have made their way into the night thoughts of Molly Bloom. Mrs Bloom and Mrs Joyce share the same un-punctuated literary style, an onflowing gush of words. From the peculiar nature of his wife's letters Joyce generalised about the processes of the female mind.

Other aspects of the letters, such as the coprophilia and voyeurism, went into the making of Mr Bloom, who in his own way is also a generalisation from the particular, in this case Joyce himself. The themes of cuckoldry, of betrayal and infidelity, had now established themselves in Joyce's imagination. 1909 marks a break with the student of his earlier work and the married men of his last works. For the rest of his writing career he would redeploy the emotions aroused in these weeks into very different permuations in *Exiles,* his only play, *Giacomo Joyce,* the brief account of an affair he left unpublished, *Ulysses,* and ultimately into the nightmare epic of *Finnegans Wake.*

At the time it was not apparent that his business trip would have such results. Though they had parted after a small tiff before he went to Dublin, he wrote and promised her a special present. This was to be a set of furs. He confesses that his memory was full of images of her. Indeed Dublin disgusted him when he thought of her. Yet he brooded upon her attitudes and her harsh remarks to him as well.

Aside from the furs, he was also having a very
[58] special gift prepared. He had written out on parchment the poems of *Chamber Music* in his best calli-
graphic hand. These he was having bound up. But
these fine thoughts in Dublin were disturbed by
threats from Trieste to leave him. When she felt
fretful Nora would often be aroused to saying such
things, which she hardly meant. Her tone soon
changed to a softer one, as Joyce reported a visit
to her room at Finn's Hotel. Soon new themes
began to emerge in their letters.

Like the development of a piece of music, Joyce
was moving towards the major theme, not only of
these letters, but of his later writing. The letters
are shocking, nevertheless at the close (as he
writes in one of them) 'a faint hymn is heard rising
in tender worship from the dim cloisters of my
heart.' Compared with her 'splendid generous love'
for him, his love for her must, he thinks, seem 'very
poor and threadbare'.

At Christmas he sent out her Christmas present,
which had at last been finished. It was indeed an
elaborate and handsome thing. He had written out
the poems of *Chamber Music* in his finest hand on
large sheets of parchment. These he had had bound in
cream leather, stamped with the Joyce arms on the
back and his and Nora's initials entwined on the
front. A beautiful book, he hoped it would always
recall for Nora the happiest days of their early love
and how hard won their relationship was.

> Perhaps this book I send you now will outlive both
> you and me. Perhaps the fingers of some young
> man or young girl (our children's children) may
> turn over its parchment leaves reverently when
> the two lovers whose initials are interlaced on the
> cover have long vanished from the earth. Nothing

will remain then, dearest, of our poor human passion-driven bodies and who can say where the souls that looked on each other through their eyes will then be. I would pray that my soul be scattered in the wind if God would but let me blow softly for ever about one strange lonely dark-blue rain-drenched flower in a wild hedge at Aughrim or Oranmore.

Naturally enough, human nature being what it is, the explicit letters have attracted the attention of critics, but I believe the wistful note struck in this passage is more truly Joycean. In going away with Nora in 1904 he had staked a great deal upon their relationship. It was no mean feat to keep the union going through long years of hardship and suffering.

Nor should Nora be forgotten. This is easy to do, as the extant letters are all from Joyce. She remains indeed an enigmatic quantity in Joyce's life. She was now five years married to Joyce; though, of course, married is not strictly correct. She was always troubled by the fact that her's was not a real marriage, as marriage was understood by people in Galway. She seems to have had difficulty in making this clear to Jim, and in any case it would have been a difficult matter to discuss with him. Her threats to leave him, both in these letters and in later years, were one of the advantages of the situation: with them she could always bring him to heel.

Was she happy during these years? Probably not. Joyce was difficult to live with, there was very little money, the children and the housekeeping got her down. Also, the year before she had lost a child, and was to have no more. But being an Irish Catholic, her expectations of marriage would not have been high. After all her mother's had failed and Joyce's mother had suffered nearly as much. She would not

have expected much and perhaps she felt that what
[60] she got was good enough.

She was by nature an amorous person and Joyce responded with enthusiasm. But having been brought up in Galway, she also had a puritanical streak. What they enjoyed so much she felt to be basically something dirty and wicked. This contradiction, at the heart of so much marital tension in Ireland, should not surprise us. Eventually sexuality waned, and Joyce's drive was diverted into his writing.

These letters of 1909 were a last gesture to the fervour of youth. She had responded to Joyce's masochism by dominating him. But we should remember, when reading his fantasies, that in their small flat, shared with children and relatives, there would have been no place for exotic sexual practices. Her response to him by letter may well have been on the same level, but this is unlikely to have been the usual tenor of their marriage.

What the letters did achieve, even if they failed to revive the waning sexuality of their marriage, was to bring Joyce's fantasies to the surface. Having relieved himself on paper to Nora in such a fashion, it would now be possible for the artist in him to treat their correspondence objectively as a source of material for the thoughts of Leopold and Molly Bloom.

In the most important sense Nora answered Joyce's needs at two crucial moments in his life: the personal crisis in 1904, when he admitted that she made him a man; and after 1909, in his artistic crisis following upon the long troubles in publishing his book, of finding a way forward in his art.

6
The Tide Turns

In January 1910 Joyce returned to Trieste bringing with him yet another sister, this time Eileen, to join Eva in his household, despite his brother's outraged protests.

His return to Trieste restored the old relations between Nora and himself. Nevertheless her threats of leaving him might still be made, but nothing ever came of them. Once she went so far as to begin a letter to her mother.

'If you must begin a letter you might use a capital 'I',' said Joyce over her shoulder. 'Ah, what does it matter?' Nora replied. The letter was never sent.

Nora was a good-hearted person, who had little time for the niceties in a small flat. Eva Joyce was mortified one day when they had been setting the living room to rights that Nora lifted a chamber pot and put it up on the dresser in pride of place. Doubtless a pretty floral pattern prompted her to show it off. Eva only thought this ill bred on Nora's part. But the incident now seems to have a nice touch of Molly Bloom about it.

Eva did not care for Nora, and in this probably represented the middle-class affectations which the Joyces still retained from the old days. She thought that her brother had got himself into a false position by going away with Nora and could not get himself out of it. This hardly agrees with the facts of the matter, or indeed with Joyce's ability to get himself out of anything he wanted to get out of.

Relations with Stanislaus remained as edgy as ever. The younger brother felt himself more isolated now from his family, but was beginning to make his own circle of appreciative friends in Trieste. Yet despite the family tensions and rows, there were good times in between. In the evenings there would be excursions to the cinema or, more often, to the opera which both Nora and James loved. It was during these years in Trieste that Nora made herself familiar with the arias of many works, often quite obscure ones now long forgotten, but remembered in *Ulysses* and *Finnegans Wake*. She might well have been illiterate — by Joyce's exacting standards most people would be — but she had an instinctive love of music and song which matched well with Joyce's and which she tried to cultivate.

Happy days, little money. The Volta failing, that fortune which he hoped would support his writing still seemed as elusive as ever. He became discouraged with attempting to write at all. Maunsels were delaying over the publication of *Dubliners,* and were demanding cuts in the text which Joyce would not make. The uncertainty over his stories made work on anything else difficult, and his temper uncertain. Nora found him unbearable. After a particularly fierce row about eating and writing, the manuscript of his novel ended up on the fire and had to be rescued by his sister Eileen.

It was about this time, perhaps in 1911, that Nora's affair, if it can be called that, with a friend of Joyce began. Roberto Prezioso was the editor of *Il Piccolo della Sera* for which Joyce wrote. He was one of their best friends in Trieste, and had been very helpful to Joyce in many ways in the past. While Joyce was away in Ireland, he had fallen into the habit of calling on Nora in the afternoons. She was naturally flattered by the attentions of this handsome figure.

At first Joyce does not seem to have objected to these visits. Perhaps he was flattered that men were still interested in his wife. Nora thrived on the attention. But when Prezioso attempted to become something more than a friend, Joyce stepped in. He expostulated with his friend on the Piazza Dante — a scene doubtless selected by Joyce from his interest in Dante. Joyce was to dream years later of Prezioso weeping.

Our knowledge of this affair is only second hand, and though a friend of their Paris years was to speculate about the possibility of Nora having strayed in the more amorous climate of the south as a younger woman, he had no real evidence. It is a moot point, but adds something to the well of experience from which Joyce drew Molly Bloom and her cuckolded husband.

Joyce's attempt to treat his life as a work of art fed back into his writing. Much of his play *Exiles* — 'a rough and tumble between de Sade and Freiherr von Sacher Masoch' — was drawn from his experiences of Nora's relationships with other men in Ireland and Austria. Yet he remained uncommonly jealous, and continually tempted fate by allowing such approaches, despite Nora's obvious loyalty and lack of inclination for affairs.

In 1912 Nora, now eight years away from home, decided to take the children back to Galway for a holiday. It was planned that she should travel ahead with Lucia and send back some money for Joyce to follow with Giorgio. This trip would allow Joyce to look into the delays over *Dubliners* in person, as well as providing the honeymoon he had promised during the excitement of 1909. There was, of course, the small matter of Nora's lack of a wedding ring. Joyce forbade her to wear one but she ignored him. Rather than distress her mother, she wore a ring in Galway, whatever Joyce might feel about it.

Nora left for Dublin, where she duly made inquiries [64] about the book at Maunsels. She brought John Joyce and one of the boys with her but they allowed George Roberts to avoid the issue. So she went down to Galway, leaving the business to the men. Meanwhile Joyce was unhappy to have heard nothing from her. He became slightly hysterical and after a sleepless night set out with Giorgio without waiting for the money to come.

In Dublin he saw Roberts briefly, then hurried after Nora. She was delighted at his sudden arrival. Their holiday was very enjoyable. Much of the time, however, Nora hardly stirred from her mother's hearth, but James was out all the time, rowing or cycling. One Sunday he took himself off on his bicycle to visit the graveyard in Oughterard where he had imagined Michael Bodkin was buried. It was just as he had imagined it would be when he was writing 'The Dead', and he was morbidly satisfied to find a headstone bearing the name J. Joyce as well. Another day however he did go to see Bodkin's actual grave, for he later describes it. The visit inspired him to write poetry again on his return to Trieste.

In the middle of August Joyce returned to Dublin to renew the struggle with Roberts over *Dubliners*. Nora stayed in Galway with the children, but then came up to take digs in which John Joyce joined them. Doubtless they went to the Abbey to see the plays of Yeats and Synge, as he had promised her. 'You have a right to be there because you are my bride,' he had written to her before she arrived, 'and I am one of the writers of this generation who are perhaps creating at last a conscience in the soul of this wretched race.'

But the guardians of the Irish soul, in the person of George Roberts and his printer, were not anxious for Joyce's moral vision to come before the people he was writing about. Even after extensive deletions and changes had been discussed, Roberts would still [65] not bring out the book for fear of the consequences. Joyce tried to have the book published by himself, but this did not come off, as the printer would not release the sheets to him. On the morning of 11 September 1912 the sheets were at last destroyed at a loss of £57 to the printer. Moral scruples have seldom been carried further by a Dublin businessman.

And that was the end so far as Joyce was concerned. Bitterly disappointed, he left Dublin that night. This was to be his last sight of his country and his native city. He was done with Dublin: henceforth he would travel there only in imagination. He was filled with a final sense of exile, and this, as Padraic Colum suggests, was what fired the creativity of the following years. Like Dante, 'midway in this our mortal life', his senses sharpened by isolation, he would create his own divine comedy. These last journies back in 1909 and 1912 had provided him with the themes and much of the material for the rest of his creative life.

On the way back to Trieste, in the train between Flushing and Saltzburg, he scribbled out on the back of the Maunsels contract a diatribe against his enemies which he called *Gas from a Burner*:

> ... This lovely land that always sent
> Her writers and artists to banishment
> And in a spirit of Irish fun
> Betrayed her own leaders, one by one.
> 'Twas Irish humour, wet and dry,
> Flung quicklime into Parnell's eye ...

He offered the book next to Elkin Matthews, hoping that it might be possible to take advantage of the curious history of the book itself and of the topical interest in Dublin which the Great Lock-Out of 1913 aroused. It was turned down. Mills and Boon (now better known for their romances: a strange conjunction this might have been) also refused it. Some forty publishers in all, Joyce later claimed, rejected the book.

Soon after their return from Ireland in 1912, Joyce began conducting, perhaps as a counterpart to Nora's relationship with Roberto Prezioso, an ironic, superficial and altogether elevated affair with one of his prettier girl pupils. His account of his feelings for this dark lady is contained in the alusive and elusive prose of *Giacomo Joyce*. Nora may well have guessed at his preoccupation, but there is no direct evidence that she did. The affair, such as it was, petered out in the summer of 1914.

As with Emma Clery, the girl who passes so briefly through *A Portrait* and *Stephen Hero,* there is some difficulty about the identity of this girl. But whoever she was, she gave Joyce another image of the pure virginal personality which aroused him. These virgins that inhabit the pages of Joyce's fictions, however rich of flesh and blood they may have been in real life, are pale insubstantial figures beside his married women. Emma Clery is nothing against Molly Bloom, Beatrice Justice (in *Exiles*) nothing against Bertha Rowan. These wives owed much to Nora.

Joyce's attempt to fictionalise Nora began soon after their arrival in Trieste, when they filled up legal documents giving her name as Gretta Greene. From this it was only a short step to the name of Gretta Conroy in 'The Dead'. But she, however, is seen only through the eyes of her huband. In *Exiles* Joyce was to attempt a dramatic portrait of a marriage at a moment of crisis. In Molly Bloom the cycle is completed, with a completely subjective creation of the wife's view of the husband.

Joyce began sketching out *Exiles* in November 1913, and the play itself was written during the course of the next year or so, being finally finished in September 1915 in Zurich. This was Joyce's most important exploration of the female mind since he had written about Nora's love for Michael Bodkin in 'The Dead'. In this play about an Irish writer's return to Ireland and his 'betrayal', there are many elements drawn from Joyce's own life.

A summary of the plot does little to make clearer the complexities of the play, which has generally been thought of as Joyce's one failure, but which has taken on new stature since the celebrated production in London in 1970 directed by Harold Pinter. Set in the summer of 1912, the play deals with the relations between Richard Rowan, a Joyce-like writer newly returned from abroad, his wife Bertha, Beatrice Justice, a music-teacher who had been involved with Richard nine years before and Robert Hand, an old friend of Richard who attempts to seduce Bertha at a cottage which he and Richard had once shared.

But Joyce is interested not so much in mere adultery, but in the relations between the two men and the two women as well. As he himself observed, the elements of de Sade and Masoch are important. Robert writes an article on Richard's return which is actually a veiled attack upon him as a betrayer of his country: a dramatic version of Joyce's experiences in Ireland that same summer. The play closes on a rehearsal of Richard's doubts and Bertha's appeal to him to come back to her.

Even from this meagre outline, it is clear that many parts of the play are transformations of events in Joyce's life in Ireland and Italy. The notes for the play were written late in 1913: early in 1914 Joyce began work on *Ulysses* by drafting 'preliminary sketches for the final sections'. In other words, working on from *Exiles* he began *Ulysses* with Molly Bloom. The character of this Celtic woman grew out of the character-type he had been developing through Gretta [68] Conroy and Bertha Rowan. Joyce intended the conclusion to be an affirmation of love, whatever peculiar form it took.

This creative drive was being fed at last by some success. In 1913 Ezra Pound wrote to Joyce with the encouragement of Yeats (whom Joyce had told about the fate of his book in Dublin). Pound asked if Joyce had any manuscripts for publication, as he was interested in new material for a London magazine with which he was connected. So it was that the new version of his novel, now finally entitled *A Portrait of the Artist as a Young Man,* began appearing serially in the *Egoist* in February 1914. Grant Richards (after some dispute about Joyce's use of a continental dash rather than the inverted Anglo-Saxon commas in dialogue) published *Dubliners* in June 1914, a long decade after the first of the stories had been conceived and written.

But this outburst of literary endeavour was interrupted by the outbreak of a general European war in August 1914. So just as Joyce was beginning to receive the recognition he had striven for, society was thrown into an unprecedented upheaval. The institution where he was now teaching was closed, and his private pupils were called up for military service. As British subjects the position of the Joyces was difficult. After giving a pledge of his neutrality to the Austrian authorities, Joyce and his family were allowed to leave the Austrian Empire for the safe haven of Zurich in Switzerland. Stanislaus, however, was interned because of his more outspoken views.

In Zurich, apart from giving his usual language lessons, Joyce was partly supported in 1915 by money from the Royal Literary Fund which was granted to him at the request of Yeats, Pound and Edmund Gosse. In 1916 he received a civil list pension of £100 from the British treasury. This enabled him to complete *Exiles,* but he failed to find anyone to stage it.

Life in Zurich was as difficult as it had been in Trieste in the early days. Their first flats were cramped and sordid and infested with mice, which disgusted Nora. In 1915 when they arrived in Zurich, Joyce was thirty-three, Nora thirty-one and the children ten and eight. They were now personalities in their own right and this in itself was enough to create a different emotional climate in the household. In the family circle they talked Italian, but in school they had to learn the local Swiss dialect. Their disrupted lives were to have unhappy consequences.

In 1916, an eventful year for Ireland, *A Portrait* was at last published in December by Ben Huebsch in New York. Harriet Weaver, the publisher of the *Egoist,* was unable to find any firm in England who would bring out the book without textual changes. So she herself brought out a British edition, with American sheets, in 1917 under the *Egoist* imprint. Once again the reviews were laudatory.

Like all his books *A Portrait of the Artist as a Young Man* had had a difficult birth, not to say a traumatic one. It had its origins in that vast but abandoned work *Stephen Hero* begun in the early months of 1904. Dissatisified with the first version, Joyce began a new version which he finished in 1914. As with his short stories, he carried the narrative from childhood into early manhood, altering the nature and tone of the prose, making each episode more suitable in its treatment to its period of life. Thus the book opens with the childish burblings of the infant, and comes to a close with the carefully argued dialectics between Stephen and Lynch on aesthetics and Stephen and Cranly on religion. The book thus lays out the emotional, intellectual, artistic and religious experiences of a young Dubliner at the turn of the century. Reading it has been an enlightening experience for two generations of other young Dubliners, so closely are experiences of school, college and family recreated.

In reviewing the book on its first publication, H. G. Wells (with his usual bitter distaste for the Roman Church) took Joyce's account to be typical. In fact it is not. Many of Joyce's experiences were unusual and quite peculiar to himself. For instance during a period of religious fervour, Stephen sniffed stale urine to mortify his senses as a penitential exercise. Needless to say, no Jesuit confessor would have approved of such a perversion. But no confessor is mentioned. Joyce lived his religion, like his art, alone and without support.

Nevertheless there are many other passages in the book, such as the sermons on Hell, which strike not only a chord of recognition but one of dread. Anyone who has sat through such a retreat at a Jesuit school cannot read Joyce in a disinterested way. Thomas Merton has related how merely reading these passages inspired his own vocation, such was the shock. In the novel Joyce exposes the raw nerves of real life, still twitching under the effect of his sharp prose. The experience is unpleasant, but ultimately rewarding.

The book, however, was intended to be 'a portrait of the artist' and the passages on aesthetic theory (whatever their effect on some readers) were an essential part of Joyce's purpose. Given the nature of the experiences he had lived through, how was the artist to reclaim such a life for the purposes of literature? In its presentation of these experiences the book becomes its own answer to the problem. Yet *A Portrait* was only a partial answer. It was *Ulysses* that tried to confront all aspects of life.

In 1916 Joyce's chronic financial difficulties were assuaged by the first of a long series of grants of money from Miss Weaver. At first these gifts were anonymous, and for some years Joyce was mystified by the identity of his patron. Though she was a member of the Communist Party, Miss Weaver was also a wealthy woman. Her money was of little personal use to her. Some went into ventures such as the *Egoist*. Then with heroic altruism she supported and helped the Joyces for decades to come. Joyce had no truer friend, for her friendship was truly disinterested. Unlike many of his associates, she had nothing to gain from Joyce. He was deeply grateful to her, for her help came at a critical time. Her attitude contrasted sharply with the rejections Joyce had suffered elsewhere, both in the past and in the future.

Bolstered by these gifts Joyce almost gave up the language lessons which had been his economic mainstay for so many years. Some pupils he kept on, but more in a spirit of friendship, because of the interesting conversation they supplied. He threw himself into the café life of Zurich, then crowded with artists and political refugees of all kinds and shades, including Tristan Tzara and Lenin. And, of course, into the continuing composition of *Ulysses*.

Society in Zurich was very mixed and cosmopolitan, as it had been in Trieste. This suited Joyce. One of his friends was an English painter named Frank Budgen, then working in the British embassy. He and Joyce met regularly in the Pfauen café, and as often in Joyce's flat. Always *Ulysses* was a topic of conversation. Nora was afraid that Joyce would bore Budgen stiff with the book. Later Budgen was to write one of the first books about *Ulysses,* giving an entertaining account of its creation.

In 1918, when he began to receive yet more money from a patron, this time the wealthy American Mrs Harold McCormack, a Rockefeller heiress, Joyce was becoming more confident of his position in

Zurich. The Joyces were also friendly with an English [72] couple named Sykes, Nora being happy to have someone which whom she could talk English. A drama group was set up to put on plays in English as a small contribution to the Allied war effort, by bringing British culture to neutral Zurich. Joyce was made manager of the company. He saw this as a way of making some return for his civil list pension. Among the plays they staged was Synge's *Riders to the Sea* in which Nora played a part, the other actors being coached by Joyce to imitate her correct Connaught accent. But this enterprise fell apart in recriminations over a pair of trousers and who should pay for their purchase for a part in a Wilde play. This led to a law suit — and much later provided the basis in fact for Tom Stoppard's amusing play about Joyce in Zurich, *Travesties*.

Joyce's eyes now began to trouble him. In 1917 he had to have the first of many operations at Locarno, where he was forced to spend three months. This was the beginning of the long struggle to retrieve his failing sight by means of surgery. Health might fail him, but he was surely making a mark. That year saw the publication of eight of his poems in the distinguished little Chicago magazine *Poetry,* to which Ezra Pound had introduced him. With the publication of his books, and hopes of staging his play, he had become in a short time a recognised and important figure in the new literature of the day.

By the time the war ended Joyce's career had begun to acquire a momentum that was to carry him forward to notoriety and even fame of a peculiar and popular kind.

7

Ulysses

By now *Ulysses* was well advanced. In his memoirs, Joyce's friend Frank Budgen has described not only how Joyce passed his time in Zurich, but also how much of the novel was conceived and written.

Joyce was able to draw not only on the material which he had worked up in his earlier works, but on nearly every titbit that came his way. Budgen recalls that Joyce would note down the words of a song, a phrase, an arcane historical fact or piece of recondite sexual lore, all of which would be found a place in the book he was working on.

Nor did he refrain from attempts to recreate the sensations of past experiences. One such recreation which fed the novel was Joyce's affair with a young lady in his neighbourhood. This affair (unlike earlier ones of the same kind) is documented by letters and by the recollections of Frank Budgen.

In the late autumn of 1918 the Joyce flat was at 29 Universitätstrasse which backed onto 6 Culmannstrasse. One evening Joyce observed across the back garden a young lady in the apartment opposite. She was at that moment in 'a small but well-lighted room' in the act of pulling the chain. His 'cloacal' obsession aroused, he decided to seek her out.

One evening early in December as she was about to enter her apartment house, Joyce passed by in the street. Feigning great astonishment, he went up and spoke to her. With an elaborate charade, he pretended

to be surprised, but she reminded him of a girl he had
[74] once seen and never forgotten, standing on a beach in
his native land. But this reference to the celebrated
passage in *A Portrait* meant nothing to her, she later
revealed, as she never read the book.

After this they exchanged a few words in the street,
and he began writing to her. The affair went on for
some months. Martha Fleischmann (for such was her
name, he learnt) had a protector. After a few letters
from him imploring her interest, she asked him up to
her flat. Her protector, an engineer, was often away
and Joyce would not have to encounter him.

The relationship progressed. He told her about
himself and about his friends, such as Budgen. Over
tea she would sit by the fire, sometimes in her night-
dress, while he discussed at length those particular
items of female underclothing in which he was
always so interested. He gave her copies of his books.
He also sent her a postcard from 'Odysseus' to
'Nausicaa', and used in his letters the disguising
Greek 'e' which Bloom used in his letters to Martha
Clifford in *Ulysses*.

Martha was dark and sallow, and Joyce fondly
imagined that she had Jewish blood: actually she came
from a wealthy old Swiss family. But like Gertie
McDowell, whom Bloom admires on the beach at
Sandymount, Martha had a limp.

On his birthday in 1919, Joyce invited her to visit
Budgen's studio. Great preparations were made for
this special occasion. First the studio had to be
prepared, Budgen even going to the trouble of sketching
some mountainous female to please Joyce, and
hopefully arouse the lady. A Jewish candelabra was
borrowed also, it being Candlemas.

When all was ready, Joyce hurried off for Martha.
When she arrived Budgen thought her agreeable, 'but
no great beauty' with high breasts and a broad

bottom. The studio was admired. The drawings duly received their smirking tribute when pointed out by [75] Joyce. Then the oddly assorted couple left, leaving Budgen to tidy up.

Joyce later had to explain that he had wanted the candlestick for 'a black mass': privately he told Budgen that he had explored that night the coldest and hottest parts of a woman's body.

The affair soon petered out, though Joyce kept in touch with Martha on later visits to Zurich. He also gave her an autographed copy of *Chamber Music,* that significant text for his emotional life.

It was all very well for Joyce to conduct his research into female hearts and parts in this manner, but Budgen was not pleased to be privy to his secrets. 'But, you know,' Joyce told him, 'if I permitted myself to be under any restraint in this matter it would be spiritual death to me.' He could not deny himself the experiences life brought his way without renouncing his art. This he would never do.

This affair was clearly not his first: *Giacomo Joyce* suggests an infatuation with a girl in Trieste before 1914. And earlier there was the girl on the beach, and the original of Emma Clery, the girl sought out at the Gaelic League. All belong to the same type, their girlishness contrasting to solider virtues of his wife. They are the contrasting models for Bertha and Beatrice in *Exiles.* He wanted Nora also to have an affair, as she tearfully told Budgen soon after this, 'so that he might have something to write about'. For Joyce his private life was an essential source of literary material. These experiences poured into the making of *Ulysses.*

The novel began to be serialised in *The Little Review* in New York from March 1918 to 1920. In May 1918 *Exiles* was published in London by Grant Richards, and in New York by The Viking Press, with

which Ben Huebsch was now associated. The play
[76] appeared with none of the traumatic difficulties
that had stalled *Dubliners* or were to dog *Ulysses*.
During 1919 the *Egoist* in London began to run episodes from *Ulysses* also. But the forces of reaction
were gathering: a court injunction prevented *The
Little Review* from completing its serial, and it
became clear that volume publication both in America
and Britain was going to be a difficult matter.

To the creation of the new book everything was
germane to Joyce. It was just because the material he
was working up was so varied that he had to have a
firm structure for the book at the back of his mind.
The parallel with the adventures of Odysseus, the
connection of the various chapters with a particular
art, colour and organ of the body was an elaborate
scheme for ordering the material. Many critics have
devoted themselves to teasing out the significance of
this scaffolding, but for the ordinary reader it must
be of small interest compared with the effect created
by the final picture of life lived in all its variety.

Some of the materials Joyce used have given the
book a false reputation, both for difficulty and obscenity. But *Ulysses* is neither difficult nor obscene. A
complete reproduction of life in all its aspects, from
the refined and intellectual to the vulgar and sexual,
was what Joyce was attempting to achieve. The novel
is built up around the wanderings of Stephen Dedalus
and Leopold Bloom, a son in search of a father, and a
father in search of a son.

The affair between Blazes Boylan and Mrs Molly
Bloom provides a theme which haunts Bloom's mind
during the day, just as Stephen is haunted by the
demanding ghost of his dead mother. Naturally we do
not see much of this affair — that is not Joyce's
method. However, in the celebrated final section of
the book, which is taken up with the rambling night

thoughts of Molly, the events of their lives as well as the long day are passed in review.

John Fowles has remarked that we never learn from the classic Victorian novels what people said to each other in bed. Joyce tells us this and more. It was this breaking with literary convention in the matter of style and social convention in the matter of content that gave the book its immediate impact in the 1920s. Inevitably the passage of time has made much of what *Ulysses* contains seem tame stuff indeed. But Irish readers should always bear in mind that Joyce's book gives a very just idea of how real lives were lived in Dublin in 1904, and that this picture should be remembered when the more conventional ideas of our school history books are presented as authentic versions of the past.

Joyce finds room for some significant events such as the founding of Sinn Fein, an epidemic of cattle disease and the opening of the Abbey Theatre. But these public events find their significance altered by being part of a pattern dominated by the thoughts and feelings of an artist on the one hand, and a common man on the other.

Joyce had an almost complete contempt for the merely bourgeois literature of the day. In many ways it was untrue to life. If an artist was to be true to himself he had to be true to life, as he had experienced it. But such truth is often painful, as Joyce realised, and many readers then and since have not cared to face such painful truths. In this sense Joyce has never gone out of date: *Ulysses* is new every day.

Much of the material for the book Joyce accumulated by obsessive research into documentary sources, hence the seeming exactness of names and places. P. W. Joyce's *Irish Names of Places* had been a celebrated book of the previous generation: James Joyce's names of Irish places was to become even more famous.

But aside from the results of his own researches Joyce
[78] also made use of his own experiences in writing the
book. Thus it is limited socially to those Dublin circles
with which he was most familiar. This is the real Dublin but not the whole Dublin.

In October 1919 Mrs McCormack cut off her allow-
ance to Joyce under what he considered to be sus-
picious circumstances. (She was actually applying to
him advice which C. G. Jung had given her about a
painter she also supported, but who would not paint.)
Joyce had a habit of seeing plots against him in the
slightest of reverses.

At the end of the war the Joyces hurried back to
Trieste. This was in October 1919. They found they
were not entirely welcome. Brother Stanislaus, released from internment, was as determined as ever
on creating a life of his own. Nor did he care for what
he had read of *Ulysses*. The city too had changed.
Under Austrian rule it had been a bustling and important port. Now under international control, the
reason for its existence had vanished. In Italy Mus-
solini had founded the Fascist Party, and Joyce's old
literary idol D'Annunzio had taken to the life of action, leading an invasion of nearby Fiume. Trieste
was alive with nationalism and politics, and the streets
seethed with threatened revolution. This was not the
sort of heady atmosphere that Joyce enjoyed. It was
all too reminiscent of Ireland, then trembling on the
verge of a new revolution itself. In Trieste a writer
could get killed.

After a fretful year teaching at his old institution,
which had now been raised to the status of a university,
Joyce arranged to meet Ezra Pound in Switzerland.
After that they might take a holiday in England. There
he hoped to finish *Ulysses*. When they got to Switzerland, he thought they might stay a week or so in Paris.
So he resigned his job and they closed up the flat in

Trieste. In the early summer of 1920 Joyce and Nora set out for the city they had planned to live in back in [79] 1904, Paris, the city of all those early dreams.

In Paris Joyce was at the cultural centre of Europe at long last. Neither Dublin nor Trieste could have been so described in the 1920s. But Paris was the focus of many new and exciting literary experiments, mainly by young expatriates from America and Britain.

When the Joyces arrived in Paris on 8 July 1920, they intended to stay a week. They remained for twenty years. In a sense their arrival was an end to exile. Joyce was recognised as a true master of his times. Nora and the family were able to live in comfort. And though their lives were still fraught with difficulties, they were of a different kind to the complete poverty that had enveloped them in Trieste.

The great problem that faced Joyce was the completion of *Ulysses*. In New York *The Little Review* had by now been prevented from continuing the serialisation of the book after the Society for the Prevention of Vice had claimed that the novel was pornographic and had obtained a court order against the magazine. Such censorship at home had driven young American writers to Europe seeking a freer atmosphere. This they found in Paris, where their dollars went further and printers were cheaper.

This atmosphere also suited Joyce, and the plans for London were set aside. Joyce the family man was eminently respectable however, and utterly bourgeois in his habits. Paris, with its elegant shops and restaurants, suited Nora and the children well enough. Or so it seemed at the time.

Finishing *Ulysses* was an incredible task — he continued to expand and revise the text right up to the week of publication. But writing the book was simpler than publishing it. Commercial publishers failing him yet again — obscurity and obscenity were pleaded —

in 1921 Joyce agreed to the publication of *Ulysses* in Paris by Sylvia Beach, an American lady who ran a celebrated bookshop called Shakespeare & Co. This literary enterprise was also sponsored by Adrienne Monnier, who owned another literary bookshop, and by Ezra Pound and the French writer Valery Larbaud, who introduced the Irish writer through lectures to French readers.

After many tribulations *Ulysses*, in two stout, square, bluebound volumes, was at last published on Joyce's birthday in 1922. The book received both acclaim and denigration; Joyce did not really care which so long as the book was discussed. It was also a commercial success and several printings of the Paris edition were soon sold out. Sales were seriously affected in Britain when copies were seized and burned by the Customs at Folkestone: some 500 copies of the first edition went in this way.

From the first *Ulysses* has enjoyed a reputation for being difficult and obscure. Once merely owning it was such an achievement that many people thought reading it unnecessary. When it became the object of complex critical commentary any thought of readers merely enjoying it seemed to be forgotten. However the structure of the book is simple enough, and the content never rises much above the events of ordinary experience.

The book is divided into eighteen chapters or episodes, arranged in three parts, of three, twelve and three chapters each. Each chapter deals with a specific hour of the day and a specific theme. The structure of book was planned to follow the adventures of Odysseus in the *Odyssey*, but these Homeric parallels can be safely left for further readings. The book had its origins in a short story, 'Mr Hunter's Day', which Joyce had thought of including in *Dubliners*, but which got no further than the title. Mr Hunter had been a cuckolded Dubiner who had actually picked up Joyce after a fight in the street, dusted him down and seen him home. The story was to have followed Mr Hunter through his daily round until this encounter in the evening. Transforming the idea into a novel Joyce was able to enlarge the scope of the theme.

The first three chapters deal with Stephen Dedalus, whom we find living with his friends in the tower in Sandycove, much as Joyce himself had done in 1904. Stephen, feeling rejected, resolves not to sleep that night in the tower. His day is to be entwined with that of Mr Bloom, to whose house he comes at night. The second chapter shows Stephen teaching at a school in Dalkey, and the third walking back into Dublin along Sandymount strand. The themes of these chapters are respectively theology, history and philology; God, Man and Words: subjects of perennial interest to Joyce himself. But these chapters are merely introductory.

The main part of the book opens in chapter four with Mr Bloom preparing breakfast. His day will include a bath (which Joyce remarked was an unusual event in Dublin in 1904), a funeral of an old friend, visits to a newspaper, to fix up about an advertisement and to the National Library, wandering in the city streets, a musical interlude in the Ormond Hotel, a political discussion in Barney Kiernan's pub, the tumescent contemplation of a girl's underclothes on Sandymount beach, a call to Holles Street hospital where he meets Stephen, and an excursion into Nighttown from which he retrieves the young man.

The closing chapters follow Bloom and Stephen back by way of a coffee stall for cabmen in Beresford Place to Bloom's house in Eccles Street. The last chapter then reverts to Mrs Bloom, whose adultery with Blazes Boylan has run as an undercurrent in her husband's mind all day.

The plot of *Ulysses* (if it may be called that) is

simple enough. The treatment, however, is complex.
[82] The narrative style of each chapter is adapted to the subject and theme of that chapter. This technical virtuosity comes to a head in the Holles Street chapter. Bloom calls into the hospital to inquire after a friend who is expecting a baby, and finds Stephen drinking with a group of doctors, all simple enough to narrate. Except that Joyce choses to narrate his 'information', which deals with foetal development and birth, by means of a narrative which passes through the various stages of the development of the English lauguage itself. A chapter which begins with Anglo-Saxon and ends in a welter of contemporary slang is bound to provide difficulties even for the most diligent and perceptive of readers.

But for much of the book the difficulties are not caused by the problems of understanding what is said, but in taking in the levels of associative meaning with which Joyce has loaded the narrative. Here the Homeric parallels allow him great scope, in making the events of this ordinary day echo with the struggle of mythology. From this we might understand that the Greek hero was perhaps an ordinary enough man beneath his boasting. Or we might come away convinced that in the ordinary life of Dublin there was room for heroic gesture. By reducing the pretensions of the heroic, Joyce elevates the worthiness of the everyday.

So Joyce brought to conclusion a work which had begun as a short story some sixteen years before and on which he had worked for some eight years at a single stretch. The actual conclusion of the book, written in the autumn of 1921, was a remarkable evocation of the female mind on the edge of sleep:

> O and the sea the sea crimson sometimes like fire
> and the glorious sunsets and the figtrees in the
> Alameda gardens yes and all the queer little streets

and pink and blue and yellow houses and the rose-
gardens and the jessamine and geraniums and cac-
tuses and Gibraltar as a girl where I was a Flower
of the mountain yes when I put the rose in my hair
like the Andalusian girls used or shall I wear a red
yes and how he kissed me under the Moorish wall
and I thought well as well him as another and then
I asked him with my eyes to ask again yes and then
he asked me would I yes to say yes my mountain
flower and first I put my arms around him yes and
drew him down to me so he could feel my breasts
all perfume yes and his heart was going like mad
and yes I said yes I will Yes.

8

Paris: Work in Progress

Following the publication of the book which she had done much to inspire, but which she never read, Nora felt it would be a good time to visit her mother in Ireland. Miss Weaver had just made Joyce a present of £1,500 (making a total of £8,500 that she had given him over the years) and he himself fancied a trip somewhere to recover from his exertions over *Ulysses*. Now that there was some money to hand, Nora insisted on Ireland. Joyce was not so keen. He was no admirer of the new Irish Free State, even though Desmond FitzGerald, the Minister for External Affairs, wished to nominate him for the Nobel Prize.

Nora was fixed on the trip, however, and they had a fierce row, in which many of the minor resentments which had built up recently over her detached attitude to his writing came to a head. After heated words on both sides, Nora and the two children departed for Ireland on 1 April 1922. She may even have had some inchoate plan in mind to settle in Dublin or Galway with the children.

After short stays in London and Dublin they eventually arrived in Galway. From there she wrote and wired to Paris for money. Joyce responded with a desolate letter and the cash. However in Galway all was not well. The country was poised on the brink of a civil war between the army of the new Free State and the irregular Republican forces who did not accept the terms of the Anglo-Irish treaty. The street in which

they were staying lay between the two sides and became the scene of a dispute between the government [85]
troops and the irregulars. Nora was frightened. They
packed their bags and left. On their way back to Dublin the train was fired upon. George took this all lightly
enough, but in fact the situation was even more serious
than Nora imagined. In a few months the Republican
opposition to the treaty had plunged the country into
a blood bath.

Joyce was shaken by this incident, and even tried
to send a plane to rescue them from Galway. His sus-
picions about Ireland were confirmed. He was to re-
fuse future invitations even from people such as Yeats
and Shaw. He was afraid for his life, perhaps not without reason. After all, his two college friends Francis
Skeffington and George Clancy had both been mur-
dered in the troubles, Yeats' house had been fired
upon, and Oliver Gogarty had barely escaped with his
life after being captured by Republicans. Some crank,
such as the one who had sneered at his son on the
street in Galway, 'How does it feel to be a gentleman's
son?', might well have taken a potshot at a figure as
notorious as Joyce.

Joyce was frantic while they were away, but soon
they were safely back with him in Paris. Nora now
agreed that Ireland was not perhaps the safest place for
the Joyces. The summer of 1923 was spent at Bognor
in England: nowhere could be further from revolution.
There Nora's younger sister came to stay with them.
Joyce took to her. He asked her what they thought of
the copy of *Ulysses* that he had sent Mrs Barnacle. The
girl hesitated. 'Well, Mam says it's not fit to be read.' 'If
that is so,' he replied, 'then life is not fit to be lived.'

The tensions in Joyce's life, between himself and
Nora, between parents and children, were to be turned
to creative use. But they took their emotional toll in
many small ways.

In 1923 Joyce began work on a new book. This was
to be called *Finnegans Wake*, a title taken from the
popular ballad about the death and resurrection of a
Dublin hod-carrier who was a little too fond of his
tot. The title was a close secret between himself and
Nora. Otherwise to the outside world the strange new
creation was simply 'Work in Progress by James Joyce'.

By 1924 he was prepared to begin publishing the
first fragments of *Work in Progress* in the expatriate
literary journal the *Transatlantic Review*. Later sections appeared in other journals, until Eugene Jolas
began to publish the work almost continuously in
transition from 1927 to 1938. The work was of
its nature very difficult, but Joyce also began to be
troubled constantly by his eyes, a disability he was
never again to be of.

In March of that year Herbert Gorman's account of
Joyce's first forty years was published, both in New
York and in London. This was a public indication
that Joyce had become an established figure in the
first rank of modern writers. His reputation was made.
Already the work by which he was to be known and
widely read was complete. To a very large extent what
followed appeared to many as being out of joint with
his earlier work. Joyce, to whom the essential con-
tinuity of his life was more obvious, did not think
this, and he toiled on through illness and hardship,
emotional and financial.

Work in Progress was only part of Joyce's literary
interest in these years. More important to him were
his efforts to secure the publication of *Ulysses* in
England and America.

In 1926 much of *Ulysses* was pirated and serialised
in an American review, *Two Worlds Monthly*. American copyright law held that if a book was not produced
by American labour, within two years of publication
it passed into the public domain. This clause, intended

to protect American printers, had served only to rob European writers. An international protest signed by some 167 figures in the world of arts and letters was organised against this blatant act. Eventually the review's editor, Roth, was prevented by injunction from continuing. But this did little to advance the prospect of publishing the entire text in America, free of expurgations.

In 1927 the Joyces spent nearly three months in London, going on then to The Hague and to Amsterdam. In Paris Sylvia Beach produced *Pomes Penyeach*, Joyce's collection of his later poems. These were mainly written after those in *Chamber Music*, though the last one, 'Tilly', dated back to the death of his mother in 1903.

The following year found the Joyces in Dieppe and Rouen, Toulon and Salzburg. These trips to resorts and watering places were the ordinary round of their lives now.

There was, indeed, nothing spectacular about the Joyces' way of life in Paris. They remained as nomadic as ever, constantly moving from flat to flat, and from hotel to hotel, until at long last Joyce took out what was to be his longest lease, on a furnished apartment in the Square Robiac, off the fashionable rue de Grenelle. There they lived from 1925 to 1931, after which date there followed another series of flats, including several years in one on rue Edmond Valentin, held from 1934 to 1939.

Nora's dream was said to have been a real house of her own, with real carpets of her own on the floor. This was a dream which never came true, for she was as unsettled as Joyce and seldom liked a place for long. Even though they moved constantly, and there were trips to fashionable resorts, friends from Ireland and Britain became used to not finding them in the same flat twice, although the family seemed always to be posed against an unchanging and unremarkable bour-

geois background.

Nevertheless, with his inherent devotion to his art,
Joyce retained (so far as his health allowed) the discipline of work which he had established in Trieste.
He would sleep late and wake for coffee about ten
o'clock. The mornings were passed quietly reading
the papers when he was able to. The *Irish Times* mailed
to him from Dublin was by now essential reading, as
was the Vatican daily the *Osservatore Romano*. He did
not talk much in the mornings. Nora complained that
when lunch was served one of the few things he said
all day was 'What's this?'

After a light lunch — whatever it was, often merely
a soup — he would start work. In the early years in
Paris when his sight was still fair, he would work at
home in his own room. There he was surrounded
with back copies of his Irish papers, sheafs of manuscripts and innumerable envelopes containing notes
and jottings. Later when his sight was failing, he would
work in the afternoons with Samuel Beckett or Paul
Léon.

Joyce would finish his day's work about seven,
emerging from his workroom wearing the white jacket
which he thought cast more light on the paper. Nora
would rise to the occasion. 'Take off that thing, Jim,
you look a sight.' He would smile knowingly at whatever friend was there and settle down to his first drink
of the day. Dinner as often as not was eaten in a restaurant, usually some fashionable place on the Champs
Elysée. Joyce enjoyed the idea of buying good food.
It was some small compensation for all that dripping,
friend bread and stirabout he had once had to make
do with. But he ate little enough of what he ordered.
He enjoyed passing the evening in convivial company
in a public place, aware of the interest that passing
strangers took in the famous author. Meeting strangers

was another matter: he did not care to do that very often, though anyone from Dublin or Ireland would be welcomed for their conversation. Nora would end the evening by urging Joyce, often happy and singing, to come on home out of that.

The Joyces' way of life often surprised those who expected this master of the modern mode in fiction to live with his family in a more 'artistic' manner. But Joyce did not mix in the fashionable intellectual circles of Paris. He despised bohemians and anyone who lived that way was not very welcome in his home. One might bring one's *belle amie*, so long as it was the same girl every time. A casual pickup, however, would not be welcomed by Nora.

Joyce's health was a source of constant worry to Nora, as were her growing anxieties about Lucia. Though he enjoyed his creative work, the strain of the long and complicated labour involved in constructing *Finnegans Wake* was taking a toll of them both. On occasion she would protest in her simple and straightforward way by walking out on him and going to stay in a hotel. Joyce would come to his senses, friends would rally round, and they would go and retrieve her.

A continuing source of strain was Nora's view that their marriage was not properly — that is legally — a marriage at all. She had never been able to persuade Joyce into a ceremony and he had concocted the tale of a marriage in Trieste in 1904. Joyce had mellowed, but not enough for him to countenance a 'real' wedding.

But in 1926 she had his old friend J. F. Byrne, then on a brief visit to Paris, broach the topic. Joyce assented warmly to the idea, and Nora was happy that one cause of her worries would soon be removed. But with Byrne gone Joyce was less easy to persuade. He did nothing in haste. It was to be five years before she got her way. In the meantime there were other worries.

Joyce's eyes had been the one source of continuous ill health in the household. In 1928 he was again troubled with inflammation but this was a small matter. Nora, who had always been a model of health, was suspected of having cancer. She went into the *maison de santé* in Neuilly, where it was found she had cancer of the womb. A course of treatment followed, and the family thought she was cured. But she was not. Another operation, which she dreaded, was needed, and she had to have an hysterectomy. In March 1929 the doctors pronounced her completely cured and allowed her to return home.

Apart from Lucia's peculiar behaviour, George was also a worry. His singing career was slow to develop, and he worried his parents by an affair with a divorced American. In December 1930, however, he and Helen Fleischman were married. She was a wealthy and attractive woman, and she and Nora were soon friends.

In 1931 Nora's own hopes of marriage rose. The Joyces moved to England, planning an indefinite stay, and it was thought necessary for testamentary reasons to secure the childrens' right to his estate, to establish domicile in Britain and to marry formally.

They took a flat in Kensington and on 4 June 1931 they were married quietly in the Kensington Registry Office. This required only one day's notice and they had hoped they would escape the attention of the press. But the lists are always scanned by reporters and the papers reported the event as a matter of course. Joyce was angry and distressed. He did not like making a spectacle of himself in this way. In Galway Nora's mother had a copy of the *Sunday Dispatch* hurried round to her by a neighbour. She too was upset, feeling that the Joyces had deceived her about their marriage.

Other family affairs tumbled them about. On 29

December 1931 Joyce's father died in Dublin of heart disease and 'senile decay', an event which deeply troubled his distant son. But then on 15 February 1932, his grandson Stephen Joyce was born in Paris. This conjunction of events touched him deeply, and for the last time in his life he was moved to verse, writing the fine little poem 'Ecce Puer', which was widely published and became the final poem in his collected poetry. If the clotted twinings of his work in progress were one use of language, this simplicity was as deeply effective:

> Of the dark past
> A child is born;
> With joy and grief
> My heart is torn.
>
> Calm in his cradle
> The living lies.
> May love and mercy
> Unclose his eyes!
>
> Young life is breathed
> On the glass;
> The world that was not
> Comes to pass.
>
> A child is sleeping;
> An old man gone.
> O, father forsaken,
> Forgive your son!

His heart had gone out to the child. But he would not allow it to be baptised. But Nora, George and Helen, together with the Colums, took the child to church where Eugene Jolas stood for him. Later he was upset when he discovered what had been done, for he regarded the Catholic religion in some ways as 'black magic'.

George's marriage had not been welcomed at first by the Joyces, and Lucia was particularly perturbed by it. Now the marriage of her own parents upset her even more. She became withdrawn. Joyce's birthday in February 1932 brought the matter to a crisis. In the morning the now resentful Lucia had a fierce row with Nora. In a careless moment Nora told her not to be 'a silly bastard'.

'Well, if I am one it's you who've made me one,' Lucia shouted back. Then she picked up a chair and threw it at her mother. George intervened and calmed Lucia down. Later in the day he drove her out to the *maison de santé* in Neuilly.

This was the first mental breakdown Lucia had. She was escaping from the pressures of family life into the vacuity of schizophrenia. Yet the family passed the summer in their usual tour of resorts, visiting Zurich, Austria and Nice. The condition of Joyce's eyes now made the appointment of a proper secretary essential. The casual aid of friends was not enough. So Paul Léon came to help him with his work.

To secure the copyright in the work in the United States parts of *Work in Progress* were published in New York in 1928 as *Anna Livia Plurabelle*. And the following year the French translation of *Ulysses* was published, the first of many translations into many varied languages. Also Joyce engineered the publication of a symposium called mangificently *Our Examination round his Factification for Incamination of Work in Progress*, to which Joyce himself contributed under the name of Slingsby.

During the first four years of the 1930s Joyce threw himself with enthusiasm into promoting the career of the Irish tenor John Sullivan. Joyce having been a talented singer was eager to see a fellow-countryman do well. He also underwent more eye surgery.

In 1933 Lucia was being treated in a Swiss clinic,

so the other members of the family passed the summer on Lake Geneva so that they might be near her. This sad and troubling year was marked by the ruling in New York by Judge John M. Woolsey that *Ulysses* was not a pornographic work. The verdict was upheld on appeal, and so the way was open for the publication in New York in January 1934 by Random House of the complete text of *Ulysses*.

The contract had been won two years before by the energetic Bennett Cerf who had founded the firm, when the Viking Press failed to go ahead fearing prosecution. Cerf came to Paris to talk to Joyce, and in his eager hurry to meet him the short-sighted author was knocked down by a taxi. His injuries were slight, and he was soon able to entertain Cerf at his apartment.

After dinner there were the usual songs. Nora grew bored. She remonstrated with Joyce and a tussle began over the piano seat, each pulling one end. Nora let her end go, and Joyce tumbled over on his bottom. Some day she promised Cerf she would write her own book: *My Twenty Years with a Genius — So-called.*

Meanwhile, a book which had been the prized acquisition of many tourists in Paris now became a best seller, 33,000 copies being sold in ten weeks. Joyce had passed almost the last barrier of acceptance. In London Allen Lane at the Bodley Head delayed the publication of the British edition until October 1936, when a limited edition was issued. An unlimited trade edition appeared finally in 1937.

It is perhaps an indication of the quite different attitudes to Joyce in the British Isles that though the American edition soon became an established book with a steady sale in the Modern Library edition, the Bodley Head edition was not reprinted until 1942, after Joyce had died. Indeed it was some time before Joyce became a popular author in Britain at all.

Anticipating the American legal decision Joyce had
[94] written to Harriet Weaver that he expected England
would follow in a few years 'and Ireland 1,000 years
hence'. But in fact, by one of those peculiar chances
of life, *Ulysses* was never banned in Ireland. The book
was certainly the subject of a Customs exclusion
order (following the British and American actions in
this respect), but this was lifted in 1932. It was never
banned by the Censorship Board which was established
in 1929. How many copies were actually sold by
bookshops is not known: the manager of one well-
known Dublin shop explained to me, 'There was not
much demand for it anyway'. The book was always
obtainable, and since 1960 has been widely available.

When it was published the book was regarded by
many as obscene rubbish. It is an instance of how our
standards of discrimination have improved that it is
now taken for granted that the book should be
required reading for students of English literature,
both here and in America. The historical irony of that
word *English* would not have been lost on Joyce;
though Irish claims for his greatness must be rung
against the rock of contempt with which an earlier
generation regarded him.

9
Finnegans Wake

The life of the Joyces in the years when *Finnegans Wake* was being created with the infinite patience of a spider spinning a web from its own insides, followed the by now familiar pattern of intense literary work and grievous family troubles. As Joyce explained to a Danish friend during a brief visit to Copenhagen:

> I haven't lived a normal life since 1922, when I began *Work in Progress*. It demands an enormous amount of concentration. I want to describe the night itself . . . my book has become more real to me than reality, and everything has led to it. There are no individual people in the book — it is as in a dream, the style gliding and unreal as is the way in dreams.

That dream was largely compounded out of his family troubles. The concentration which the book required undermined his family relations. For his children life with father was another kind of night, in which their individuality was drained away as well. For his daughter the perception of reality became a problem which was something far worse than a mere literary artifice. As her father set about the destruction of the English language (as it seemed to some of his critics) Lucia Joyce was loosing hold on the grammar of life, and it was beginning to fall apart.

For George and Lucia Joyce a normal life was also impossible.

In 1934 George Joyce moved with his wife and
[96] child to New York. George was hoping to establish
himself there as a professional singer, an ambition
that echoed his father's own youth. But though pro-
moted by his father, his career came to nothing.
Joyce believed that as in Dublin, so in the great world,
influence could make genius out of mere talent.
George had talent enough, but he lacked the character which had sustained his father through years of
great adversity. Joyce suspected that his son had suffered because of the campaign being waged against
the author of *Ulysses* in some Irish-American Catholic
quarters. But this was not the reason for his son's
failure, merely an explanation of it.

George's marriage, too, was beset with problems.
Friends of the family felt he was lacking in emotional
warmth. In this he was merely reflecting his upbrin-
ging. For whatever about the ribald nature of *Ulysses,*
the Joyce family itself had become increasingly stuffy
and narrow-minded about what might be thought
proper. George's stunted emotional nature was the
corollary to his parents outbursts in 1909. His wife
suffered a mental breakdown, recovered, then relap-
sed. Eventually after the publication of *Finnegans
Wake,* for which she had prepared the elaborate
family celebration in the Joyce's Paris apartment, she
went back to America with her brother. She and
George were eventually divorced. Later he was to
marry again, to a German doctor. He died in Munich
in 1976.

For Lucia life was even more difficult. She had
been burdened by nature with a squint, about which
nothing was done. Though her features were pretty
enough, this flaw was enough to make her painfully
conscious of her appearance. This awkwardness became something more as she passed into her teens.
The Joyces' parents had strongly rooted origins;

moving across Europe as exiles their children had not. Added to this were the strained relations between mother and daughter. Nora, in the way of Irish mothers, preferred her son. Lucia resented this, and struggled to gain and keep her father's approval.

Though ill she nurtured ambitions of an artistic kind. Having failed to become a dancer (after several years of lessons), she took up book illuminations, in which she showed little of the talent her brother had for singing. Though her father was able to help her a little by finding critics to praise her work (a few may even have thought well of it), it hardly amounted to a career, let alone an outlet for her creative energies.

What had seemed to be merely the mild eccentricities of youth began to become a worry to the family in the early 1930s. By the time *Ulysses* appeared in America, she was definitely sick. In February 1932 she was removed to a nursing home: after that date she was never really well. Slowly she was overwhelmed by schizophrenia, but the family, or rather her father, refused for a long time to accept just how ill the girl was.

In 1935 she caused the family grave concern during a trip she made by herself to London, where she stayed with the ever kind Miss Weaver. From there Lucia went on to Ireland, where she was able to live with her aunt. She disappeared in Dublin for a while, and eventually was picked up by the police. Her father's old friend Con Curran, through the influence of his official position as Registrar of the High Court, was able to keep these misadventures out of the press.

For years she had been receiving treatment for various supposed conditions: what she really suffered from was being a Joyce. At root the problem was sexual. She made absurd claims of being seduced by the young men who surrounded her father. The Colums, sensing this, thought that her father should

follow the continental custom of giving her a dowry,
[98] and marrying her off. This scheme came to nothing.
Unlike her father, she had no way of creating her own
life. After the affair in Dublin even he could no
longer deceive himself about how seriously ill she
was.

Permanent treatment was needed. In 1936, the
year in which her little illuminated book *A Chaucer
ABC* was published in Paris, the month of March saw
her removed once again to a *maison de santé*. Once
she was institutionalised she 'recovered' to the extent
of becoming 'a burnt-out case'. She is now living
happily enough in a nursing home in Northampton;
attached, visitors report, to the memory of her father.

These unhappy events in Joyce's private life are the
background to the creation of his vast impenetrable
work. Was the book merely an escape from these
horrors, or was it the only way (as some imagine) in
which he could bring himself to speak about these
private events?

The family and its nature had always been one of
Joyce's central themes. His own experiences as a child
and a young man had fed his fiction with one view
which colours the stories in *Dubliners* and some
scenes in *A Portrait of the Artist* with a black loath-
ing of family life. He had expressed some of these
feelings to Nora in that letter written before they left
Dublin (see p. 36). The experiences of his own marriage had gone into the maturer views of *Exiles* and
Ulysses, culminating in a feeling of disillusioned resig-
nation. The theme of parents and children reappears
in the strange convolutions of *Finnegans Wake* in its
most elaborate form, veiled from complete understanding by the language of the book.

Those critics who saw his new book as the creation
of a madman, and spoke of its being written in the
'language of schizophrenia', were closer to the painful

truth than they realised. Joyce himself was not mad, merely tormented by doubts and uncertainties which [99] often came close to dementia. Nor was the book's language all that strange, once an attempt was made to read it aloud, preferably with a Dublin accent.

But his daughter Lucia was a schizophrenic, and she it was who spoke the genuine language of disassociation. Whereas Joyce had the consummate control of the mature artist over his material, his daughter had nothing at all with which to give shape to her life. Like the interwining patterns of the Book of Kells, the father's art and the daughter's illness weave in and out of the final years Joyce devoted to the composition of *Finnegans Wake*.

Lucia could not escape, but for Joyce and Nora there was always somewhere else to go. In 1937 they visited Zurich once more as well as Dieppe. That year also saw the publication in London of the final fragment of his new work, a pamphlet called *Storiella as She Is Syung*. In London T. S. Eliot was concerning himself not only with Joyce's literary reputation, but also providing an eminently friendly publisher. Some patience was needed at Faber and Faber to see such a difficult work through the press. At long last the new book was brought to a close in the final months of 1938.

It was now possible to assess fully this very new departure by an eminent writer. Such heroic experiments deserve respect. But on the whole it has to be admitted that the book had had a cool reception as it has been serialised over the years. Stanislaus Joyce thought it was rubbish. Old friends such as Ezra Pound and Harriet Weaver were outraged or mystified at the new direction in which Joyce's genius was taking him. Much has been made of the difficulties and obscurities of *Ulysses,* but for the most part that book was easily read and understood. This new book seemed to be all difficulties and obscurities, quite impossible to read and understand. The book seemed less concerned with meaning than with being.

Joyce himself may have been doubtful at times about his project. As he confessed to his friend in Paris, Nino Franck, during the early thirties, 'For the moment there is still one person in the world, myself, who can understand what I have written. I can't guarantee that in two or three years I will still be able to.' By 1937 he was wondering aloud: 'Perhaps it will end in failure, be a wreck of "catastrophe" such as Virginia Woolf believed *Ulysses* was; and perhaps in the years to come this work of mine will remain solitary and abandoned, like a temple without believers.' But in fact the structure is still crowded, not so much with worshippers perhaps, but certainly with eager archaeologists.

By issuing the book in parts and by organising his friends and friendly critics to write about it as it appeared in parts, Joyce had hoped to prepare the way for a full understanding of what he was trying to do. But he failed. The book remains one which only a reader capable of profound study and application could apprecaite.

Finnegans Wake was planned on the largest scale, as nothing less than a complete history of human consciousness, passing through dreamlike stages from prehistory into the neofuture. But it was also an intensely personal history, containing the inner secrets of Joyce's private life. All of this was to be encompassed by relating, more or less, a dream which a publican, H. C. Earwicker, who is the publican of the Mullingar House in Chapelizod, has one night.

Sixteen years work went into the creation of *Finnegans Wake.* Its obvious density and richly worked texture precluded it from being regarded as merely an elaborate joke. But many readers found it difficult to adjust to Joyce's claims upon their concentration and intelligence. And so the book fell into the hands of professional explicators from whom it will never (so it now seems) be rescued.

What urge brought Joyce to write his new work is unknown. We do know that he began to write it on 10 March 1923, and that a month before this he had sorted through the notes left over from *Ulysses*. That he intended the book to be a resumé of his life's work is made clear by a notebook he had begun the year before. Under the rubric of the titles of his earlier books, he had jotted down a collection of words and phrases associated in his mind with the themes of the stories and novels. Under *Chamber Music* he observes that T. S. Eliot 'ends the idea of poetry for ladies', a sharp comment on that effete collection of verses.

He began the actual book by drafting a two-page version of what critics now call 'the Roderick O'Connor sketch'. During the next eight months he drafted five more sketches, all like the first parodies of medieval literary modes, dealing with Tristan and Isolde, St Kevin, St Patrick and the Druid, and the strange compounded character created from the authors of the Gospels, Mamalujo, with whom he associates the Four Masters of Irish history. These pieces, he told Miss Weaver, were parts of the whole and would coalesce as they were worked on.

The basic tale of the book is simple enough: a dream of family life by the publican Earwicker. He has a wife and a daughter, who echo Nora and Lucia. George too finds a place in the book. The two brothers Shem and Shaun are easily seen as transformations of Joyce and his brother Stanislaus. Joyce's methods in elaborating his material drew at the same time upon his own personal experiences and the mythological history of Ireland, expressed in a

portmanteau language of his own creation, based on
[102] English.

Finnegans Wake is an historical costume drama
with many scenes and roles, from Eden to Waterloo,
from Adam to the Man Who Broke the Bank at
Monte Carlo. But all are speaking parts of his own
family. Whatever history is about, Joyce suggests that
it is basically a family romance, and there was little
that Joyce did not know by then about families or
romance.

At this level the book would have been straightforward enough. And the early parts of the book as
published in the twenties were easy enough to follow.
Then Joyce, in bringing them together, began to
elaborate the material, adding to it as he went along
from many sources such as Sheridan Le Fanu's novel
about Chapelizod, *The House by the Churchyard,*
from *Huckleberry Finn,* and from the Egyptian *Book
of the Dead.* Now passages were worked over with
great attention, and when they found their final place
in the text were worked over again. The linguistic
puns in several languages which are such a feature of
the book are intended not merely to amuse the reader
(we should always bear in mind that *Finnegans Wake*
is a funny book: Joyce kept Nora awake at night
laughing to himself as he wrote it), but to extend and
universalise what was essentially a very local and very
personal tale. Having told all, Joyce was covering his
tracks.

Burdened by his blindness and by his family difficulties, Joyce nevertheless managed to persevere with
his work and finally brought *Finnegans Wake* to a
conclusion in March 1938 with a carefully considered
deadfall on the definite article and no full stop — the
end of the book passes over into the beginning. The
text was already passing through the press and his
London publishers managed to present him with a

finished copy of the book before his birthday on 2 February 1939. He was fifty-seven.

In the end the text as published in 1939 runs to some 628 closely printed pages. *Finnegans Wake* is a deadly serious funny book, and its critical condition gives rise for concern. Readers attempting it had better be well versed in Joyce's other writings and be prepared for many years of close reading before they will begin to fully penetrate its mysteries. The book has already kept university professors busy for a generation, and there is no sign of their industry exhausting the difficulties. But the book has also provided entertainment and enchantment for those readers who have persevered with it.

The enchantment of the book can easily be sampled by a new reader in the closing passages where the river Liffey, Anna Livia herself, flows home to the sea. These passages may convince sceptics that there is a species of lyrical power in the book which can be strange yet deeply moving. Once convinced of that many will find it easier to return with the flow of the book itself to the beginning, and to attempt to obtain some handhold on the portean lineaments of the novel.

So, Avelaval. My leaves have drifted from me. All. But one clings still. I'll bear it on me. To remind me of. Lff! So soft this morning, ours. Yes. Carry me along taddy, like you done through the toyfair! If I seen him bearing down on me now under whitespread wings like he'd come from Arkangels, I sink I'd die down over his feet, humbly dumbly, only to washup. Yes, tid. There's where. First. We pass through grass behush the bush to. Whish! A gull. Gulls. Far calls. Coming far! End here. Us then. Finn, again! Take. Bussoftlhee, mememormee! Till thousandsthee. Lps. The keys to.

[104] Given! A way alone a last a loved a long the river-run, past Eve and Adam's, from swerve of shore to bend of bay, brings us to a commodius vicus of re-circulation back to Howth Castle and Environs.

10
Joyce the Writer

The completion of *Finnegans Wake,* so clearly a work beyond which it would be difficult to progress, provides a moment at which to look back over Joyce's life and to analyse the development and actual achievement of his career as a whole. He wrote nothing else after 1938, though there was a brief engagement with the idea for a book about the sea. But that was not even sketched out. The *Wake* was for Joyce, as wakes had been for generations of Irishmen before him, the occasion for a summing-up of a life.

In 1939 he was a worn out figure, the withdrawn literary saint whom Gisèle Freund photographed. The literary vagabond of 1904 was a long way in the past. But the difference was not merely one of exchanging well-made brogues for his shabby tennis shoes. In thirty-five years Joyce had managed to impose himself upon the modern consciousness in a way which even he — ever optimistic as he was as a young man — would have thought extraordinary. An outline of his life provides only a partial portrait of how this came about, for the creator of a literary work cannot always judge the impact that it will have. The private Joyce was reclusive. The public Joyce, the Joyce of literary legend, was quite another matter. His total impact was revolutionary.

In a conversation with his friend Arthur Power, Joyce confessed that he supposed he was really a

bourgeois. This would have been a term of abuse
[106] among the avant-garde who admired Joyce. And we
can now see that it was true enough of Joyce's subject matter. What else indeed could Joyce have been
given his origins and his way of life? Brighton Square
was eminently bourgeois. But being a bourgeois Irish
writer makes Joyce almost unique, in a country
where writers are often decayed gentry or sons of the
soil. In wider terms, of course, Joyce's objective
manner was far removed from the comfortable needs
of the ordinary bourgeois reader. He is not an easy
read, and never planned to be.

Joyce's last book outlined this development. In
writing *Finnegans Wake* he began his structure with
his own earlier works, suggesting that he saw each one
not as a separate work, as we have so far seen them,
but as parts of an artistic whole.

Writing to his mother from Paris in March 1903,
Joyce outlined what he hoped would be the course of
his career: 'My book of songs will be published in the
spring of 1907. My first comedy about five years
later. My "Esthetic" about five years later again.' By
some miracle, seeing how difficult he found it to have
his work accepted, Joyce kept more or less to this
scheme, for *Chamber Music,* his 'book of songs' did
indeed appear in 1907.

The publication of the collection earned him a
place in the Imagist Movement, and indeed some of
the poems do have the same quality as those of others
in that short-lived experiment. But they belonged in
reality to quite another world, quite another period.
They were a young man's poetry, full of unrequited
longings. Though the poems brought him into association with Ezra Pound and T. S. Eliot, they derived
from the lyrics of the Elizabethan age. They were
written to be sung, which gave them a special quality
lacking in most modern verse. And it is this lyrical

quality which unites them with the alusive prose of *Finnegans Wake*. The quality of sound in the passage from Joyce's last book quoted in the previous chapter has its source in these poems. It described a river; so does the opening of Joyce's first work:

> Strings in the earth and air
> Make music sweet;
> Strings by the river where
> The willows meet.

Joyce's short stories have quite a different quality. *Dubliners* had such a difficult passage into print that its disagreeable elements which so distressed the publishers with whom Joyce struggled gave it a scandalous kind of distinction. Though the stories are indeed disagreeable, they also have a distinction of another kind: a sensitive humanity which faces the little horrors of daily life. The stories are little dramas of gradual degradation which the author suggests is inevitable, but without despising his characters.

The short story arose only in the nineteenth century, from the commercial need to fill the pages of the periodicals which mushroomed with the extension of education. But what began as a mere page filler in some hands was raised to an art form. In Russia and America and Ireland, areas then on the periphery of the cultural world, the short story became an expressive form of art. Frank O'Connor, in a suggestive study of the form, has seen the short story as the voice of submerged social groups. Certainly many of the characters in Chekhov, Anderson or Joyce are submerged in their societies, nearly drowning.

The need to fill some space in the *Irish Homestead* led to the invitation from Russell to Joyce to write some stories. But Joyce made something more of the commission: he redirected the course of the short

story as an art form. He stripped away not only the
[108] façade behind which people in Dublin lived their little
lives, but he did this by stripping away all unneeded
detail. Yet the stories were elaborated with great care
as to the symbolism he employed. For instance in the
story about religion, 'Grace', he intends the three
parts into which the short narrative is divided to echo
the arrangement of Dante's *Divine Comedy*. The
toilet in the basement of the pub is the Inferno; the
recuperation of Mr Kernan and the persuasion of his
friends to go on a retreat represents Purgatory; and
the Jesuit father's talk couched in the terms of the
commercial world which a shrewd businessman would
understand is an image of Paradise. The parallels may
not be obvious to the reader, but helped Joyce
structure his story and charge its texture with significance.

The stories abound in sharp social observation. The
nasty little antics of the 'Two Gallants' are drawn
doubtless from personal experience when Joyce himself was short of money in Dublin and might well
have borrowed from a girl in employment. But this
exploitation of the girl finds a symbolic parallel in the
figure of the harp in Kildare Street 'heedless that her
coverings had fallen about her knees, seemed weary
alike of the eyes of strangers and of her master's
hands'. These techniques Joyce was to carry further
in *Ulysses* and *Finnegans Wake,* where the structure
and content depend on parallels which are not always
clear to the reader on first sight, but which build up
the total effect of the book over a period. They also
make the stories interesting to take apart again,
although that would not have been Joyce's original
intention. But once again we can see how he developed from book to book, and how the totality is a
unity.

Central to that unity is the idea of the artist. It was

with this idea, the portrayal in fact of his own development from childhood to youth, that Joyce began his work in January 1904. The impetus to write both *Dubliners* and *A Portrait of the Artist as a Young Man* belongs to that one year, when Joyce was in an important transitional phase of his life. The short stories provided a wide social context against which the development of the unique personality of the writer described in the novel can be set. In his novel Joyce merely sketches in the background against which Stephen Dedalus moves; the stories fill it out.

This double perspective has two aspects. The first is historical. The Dublin of Joyce's work is the Dublin in which much of what is now usually considered of critical importance in the history of modern Ireland was taking place. Joyce adverts too to these events, to such things as to Arthur Griffith and Sinn Fein, to George Russell and the Co-Operative Movement. But the usual, simple view of that history as the progress of inevitable events towards the present Irish state is shown up by the evidence of literature, which illustrates instead the vigorous variety of thought and feeling at all times. Thus in those years leading up to the revolution, Joyce the sceptic moves among the idealists of the time with detachment, presenting us with another, corrective view of what we have long taken for granted.

The second perspective is biographical, the personality of the artist in an anti-literary society. Again the development of personality is an essential part of the development of society as a whole. The novel suggests that for the artist exile provides the only solution. But in Joyce's case such an exile was not a complete solution as the artist could not escape from his material, the life he had known in Ireland. Thus Joyce shows how others in that society have been warped, while only the artist has been able to adjust to reality.

In writing *Ulysses,* which was developed from a
short story intended for the earlier collection, but never finished, Joyce adopted both the perspectives at the same time. Stephen re-appears — less vain and self-satisfied perhaps, but still the poet seeking some expression of life which eludes him. Joyce now introduces Mr Bloom, seeking some life which eludes his expression, and Mrs Bloom, an expression of life who expresses life in herself. In this novel a wider ambition of purpose allows Joyce to range over a wide area of personal, political, emotional and sexual expression. Even so the social range is limited: the one person from the gentry class, Haines, is disdainfully treated by both Stephen and by Mulligan — 'God, isn't he awful'. John Mahaffy of Trinity College is said to have commented on one of Joyce's early broadsides that it was the consequence of giving education to corner boys. But of course Joyce was not a corner boy: his father was a gentleman, he told the boys at Clongowes. The social range of the book is the lower middle class — no-one has much money, yet no-one is seen doing a full day's work. This slothful indigence might well reflect the Ireland of the day — there were contemporaries who thought so.

Joyce began work on *Ulysses* at the same time as he was working on his single play *Exiles.* The dramatic form was not really Joyce's true metier, and yet the play was a distinctive product of his imagination. It was a thematic recasting of certain events in his own experience, as we have already seen. It was a piece of work essential as a preliminary to the writing of *Ulysses.* The character of Archie, however, harks back to the earliest pages of *A Portrait,* that of Beatrice Justice to the figure of Emma Clery in the later part of that book, while Robert Hand and Bertha look forward to Mulligan and Mrs Bloom in *Ulysses.* Once again we can see that the play — far from being a mere sport in Joyce's work — is a central feature of it, a pivot around which his imagination swings. Such themes as friendship, loyalty, love, childhood affection and the role of the artist, as well as the intricate theme of marital infidelity, are clearly laid out here. The play is a partial expression of Joyce the married man, rather than Joyce the student.

A full expresssion of Joyce's life views was presented in *Finnegans Wake*. As I have suggested, the book can be seen as an historical costume drama in which all the roles are played by members of the Joyce family, with a great deal of doubling up such as is always needed in a small company playing beyond their means. A novel which includes the first description of television in action cannot be said to be unaware of the real world. But if the *Wake* makes something of the world, what are readers to make of *Finnegans Wake* itself?

The book has been found profoundly satisfactory by the kind of critical mind which enjoys taking a piece of work apart and showing how each part fits together. That the finished piece, rather than the process by which it is made, is the real purpose of art is avoided by these critics. *Finnegans Wake* has largely become a property of the specialists.

When Joyce was beginning the book he scribbled out in a note book jottings about his earlier works. These notes provide a kind of key to what he saw in those books, for he was often chary of commenting on his own work, unlike some other writers. *A Portrait of the Artist* was the first work he began in that momentous year of 1904, and in his notes he comments that 'every journey from Ireland is a flight into Egypt'. By this he means that it is an escape from persecution, but that a return is inevitable if the purpose of the artist is to be achieved. Under 'The Sisters' he notes down 'Arabian nights, serial stories,

tales within tales', this in itself giving a clue to the
[112] final purpose he saw the artist as having in *Finnegans
Wake*. The almost sacred idea of the artist in isolation
which he expounds in *A Portrait of the Artist* was
slowly developed through Joyce's own emotional
growth into an idea of the writer as an historian of
human consciousness. Having pared away the idea of
dramatic narrative down to almost the bare bones of
feeling in *Exiles,* Joyce in *Finnegans Wake* moves
around again to a renewed form of lyrical expression.
The end flows over into the beginning, making his life
and his art a unity.

Joyce's work can so easily be seen and is seen by
enthusiasts as a self-contained system. Dublin, Ireland,
philosophy, theology: for some Joyceans they only
seem to exist because they are important in a Joycean
context. Real people come to be referred to as
'characters in *Ulysses*'. When Dr Richard Best, one of
the most eminent Celtic scholars in the Ireland of his
period and a director of the National Library, was so
described he protested. He was not a character in fiction. He was a real man. He had a sense of propor-
tion lacking in Joyceans.

If we keep a corrrect sense of priorities, *Ulysses*
includes rather than excludes a real view of the world.
Joyce was an Irishman and that real world is an Irish
world. What does Joyce tell us about the Irish world
that we can safely add to the sum of our knowledge?

For Joyce the city and the English language are the
essential features of Ireland. This was not, of course,
a feeling shared by other men of his generation. The
countryside, where some old, toothless peasants
might speak Irish, was completely alien to him. In his
city, economic activity is of an indirect kind, for no-
one in Joyce's works makes anything. Hence the
artist, who by definition is a maker, is a lost man.
Joyce's created world, though a complete contrast

with the desired ideal rural world of many Irish pat-
riots and politicians, is actually the real world which [113]
is now coming into existence for the whole country.
The peasants of the Irish Revival, beloved of Yeats
and Pearse, belonged to a dying nineteenth-century
world. Joyce's city folk belong, in their dreams and
ideas, to the world of the twentieth century.

Joyce chose the name Stephen Dedalus for the
name of his chief created character. Daedalus in
Greek myth was the master craftsman who created
the Labyrinth, the maze at the heart of which was
hidden the dreadful secret of King Minos' wife, the
Minotaur, a monster born of shameful lust. So also
Joyce creates a maze, the pattern of his artistic work,
at the heart of which lies also a secret of sexual shame:
the shame of being born, of living, of begetting children, of lust and madness. For, as Joyce expressed it
to Arthur Power, over the city rises a miasma of sex.
Near the heart of the pattern is the schoolboy Joyce
crying with gratitude in *A Portrait* as he encounters
that secret shame in the brothel bedroom. Joyce
suggests that at the heart of the pattern, the labyrinth
of history and culture, lies the great monster. It is not
an idea to appeal to the tidy minded who construct
neat patterns from our past, but it does give the
ordinary reader a new perspective both on Dublin and
on the accepted past. James Joyce is a great writer,
but there are more compelling reasons for reading
him than mere greatness. What he says happens
simply to be true.

11

Final Years

In May 1939 the text of *Finnegans Wake* was published in London and New York. The reception was a bewildered one: in Dublin the *Irish Times* noted the title but gave the author as Sean O'Casey. Joyce was not amused and suspected a plot against him. Elsewhere critics found it hard to come to terms with what the London *Daily Herald* called 'An Irish stew of verbiage by the author of *Ulysses* with unexpected beauty emerging now and then from the peculiar mixture.' The paper might have added that like an Irish stew it was a fine nourishing meal made from the most ordinary of materials.

Though other critics wrote friendly notices, even the fragments of *Work in Progress* had not prepared them for the totally new experience of a totally new kind of book. However, as even Joyce himself admitted that the book required an ideal reader with an ideal insomnia, this was only to be expected.

At first there were few enough of these ideal readers, but over the years the work of many writers and scholars has slowly pieced together something of what the book was intended to reveal. Or rather to conceal, for artifice and cunning have been stretched to their limits in the book in an attempt to hide the meaning. What it was intended to hide remains a mystery for the future. But even now, more than forty years afterwards, it is still worth wondering whether a book which requires so much work per page loses something in the experience of reading.

In any event, in 1939 Europe and America had [115] other things to think about aside from the difficul ties of reading *Finnegans Wake*. In wartime, the book was a neutral territory which only an Irish author could afford to live in.

In April the Joyces gave up their Paris apartment and moved to a new one, and from that one to a series of hotels and lodgings. During that last summer of peace (as it turned out to be) the Joyces visited Entretat, Berne and Zurich. Joyce was depressed at the progress of the German armies across Europe. He began drinking and spending money freely. The money was, of course, from Miss Weaver: a note of his sales in America for the last six months of 1939 showed *Exiles*, 0; *A Portrait*, 0; *Dubliners*, 6. His royalty cheque for *Finnegans Wake* came to $47.45.

Joyce told Beckett, 'We are going down hill fast', a view many shared. With the outbreak of war they returned to France, staying first at La Baule, one of eight addresses during these hectic months. After a brief visit to Paris, they went to Saint-Gérand-le-Puy for Christmas with Maria Jolas, whose evacuees' school Stephen was attending. Lucia, however, was still in her *maison de santé* in Occupied France, and this was the cause of great concern to Joyce, as arrangements for her removal had become quite confused.

Clearly it was time to go. Vichy France might be technically neutral, but it was also pro-German, and no place for a British subject, even one of Irish birth. Joyce had refused the offer of an Irish passport, to which he was perfectly entitled, and this made his efforts to leave for Switzerland that much more complicated. To have gone to Ireland or America might have been possible, but neither would have pleased Joyce.

In May 1940, while Joyce was still at Saint-Gérand-
[116] le-Puy, Herbert Gorman's enlarged biography appeared. Joyce had spent a great deal of time the
previous summer making alterations in the text of
this book, performing cosmetic changes on his relations with his father, his marriage and his daughter's
illness. But the actual position of the author and his
family got worse. Joyce tried to obtain a *permit de
sortie* for Lucia to leave Occupied France but failed.
Evenually the family were forced to leave without
her, and she remained in her hospital all through the
war.

After further complications over their passports
and visas as well as money to support themselves in
exile, the Joyces returned to Zurich where they had
spent the First World War.

They arrived there on 17 December 1940 and were
soon installed in their old hotel, the Pension Del-
phine, and were busy looking for an apartment.
Joyce was content to take things easy, walking in the
afternoons with his grandson, seeing small groups of
friends in the evenings. Among a few new friends was
Professor Heinrich Straumann of the University of
Zurich who had certified his literary merit for the
Swiss Federal authorities.

Straumann met Joyce shortly before Christmas,
and asked him why he had thought of coming to
Zurich. It was like being among old friends, Joyce
explained. In any case America was not his 'cup of
tea', and 'if I have always used Ireland as a place to
escape from, why should I change now and use it as
a place to escape to?'

But Joyce did not want to discuss the war, or even
literature. Straumann changed the conversation to
music and Joyce cheered up. Joyce insisted that the
human voice, the male voice in particular, was the
most expressive and noble of instruments. Later,

talking of *Finnegans Wake,* Straumann realised that
the book should be seen in this way, as a sort of grand
opera, a musical work for voices. The Joyces spent
Christmas with the Giedions, staying late into the
night singing songs in Latin and Irish.

And it was in Zurich that Joyce was taken ill suddenly in January 1941. For years he had complained
about stomach pains, but the health of his eyes had
seemed more pressing, and these aches had been put
down to 'nerves'. On Thursday, 9 January, he took
Stephen out for a walk, from which he returned in
good form. Later he went out to see an exhibition of
nineteenth-century painting, and then on to the
Kronenhalle restaurant where there was a dinner
party to celebrate a friend's birthday. Joyce drank a
great deal of Neuchâtel white wine. When he got
home he had a stomach ache. He went to bed, but at
four a.m. on Friday 10th he woke with a fearful, intense pain in the abdomen.

His usual doctor was away. George called another,
Dr Wehrlii, who left after giving Joyce a shot of mor-
phine for the pain. Wehrlii made an error here, for
when he came the next day the symptoms had
declined. But he was dissatisfied with what he saw,
and in the evening returned with a surgeon, von
Heinrich Freysz. A man of great experience, Dr
Freysz found the symptoms equivocal, but insisted
that Joyce be taken to the Schwesterhaus Vom Roten
Kreuz at once. Writhing in pain, as Stephen later recalled, Joyce was taken away.

Next morning, Saturday 11th, Joyce was worse.
Tests revealed blood, and x-rays air, below the dia-
phragm, showing that an ulcer had perforated. By
now some thirty hours had elapsed, and the chances
of survival were slim. Nevertheless he was operated
on, and the rupture treated. Joyce seemed to rally.
He feared from the pain that he had cancer, but was

reassured by his son that this was not the case.
[118] Though he looked better on Sunday morning, he had an internal haemorrhage in the afternoon and collapsed. He passed into a coma. He died in the early hours of Monday, 13 January 1941, twenty days short of his fifty-ninth birthday. That day of the month he had always regarded as an ominous one: and so it had proved.

He was buried in the Fluntern cemetery with little ceremony. There was no representative of his country at the secular service on 15 January, but in Ireland his death was widely noticed. His immediate family spoke of his interest in religion, trying to make him sound more conventional than he was. Old friends wrote of the student they had known, the artist they had admired. In his native city, where he had justly feared the bitter tongues of envy all his life, mere personal opinions about Joyce the man now mattered little. Though he had scorned the immortality promised by his religion, his art had brought him the only kind of immortality that has any meaning to the living.

His life complete, his books ceased to be merely contemporary, and became classics of their kind.

* * *

The significance of a writer's life is larger than the mere events which a biography records. For a writer his work is his life, and often his life is his work as well. No account of Joyce's life would be complete without some discussion of Joyce's place in Irish literature.

I emphasise this point because, naturally enough, his place in modern European literature has been much discussed. In his time he belonged to the Modern Movement in English writing, and was associated with Ezra Pound (who helped to bring his work to wider notice) and T. S. Eliot (who actually published him at Faber and Faber). The Modern Movement was very conscious of its own novelty, of casting off the conventions of Victorian literary decorum. Today we can more clearly see how the roots of these writers go back into earlier traditions, of literature, religion, and philosophy. Joyce's roots were in Ireland. His relationship with the other writers of his own country is of essential importance.

Born in 1882, Joyce belonged to a generation which grew up with the Irish Revival well under way (Yeats had been born in 1865), both culturally and politically. As we have seen, Joyce was no respecter of established reputations. He cared neither for Yeats and the Abbey Theatre, nor for Arthur Griffith and Sinn Fein. At college he referred contemptously to Their Intensities and Their Bullockships — those political enthusiasts and country-born students who surrounded him. His contemporaries, both at school and at college, felt he was out of step with them. Indeed his lack of faith in a Catholic country, and his political indifference in a time of revolution, could not but make him stand out.

It is true he mellowed in his views, so that by the 1920s he was prepared to telegraph his congratulations to Yeats when he received the Nobel Prize for Literature, and to admire what Griffith was trying to do in the Free State. But he could not return to that country, no more than he could write like Yeats. Joyce was a European, a part of the main. He did not belong with an island tradition.

What had interested Joyce from his late teens was the literature of Europe; from Dante to Ibsen he took it all to himself. In writing he wanted realism always, but a realism tempered by symbolic form. It was the realism of his own writings which separates him from most other Irish writers, both of his own and other generations.

Poetry has long had a larger place than prose in the
literary traditions of Ireland. Indeed the Irish novel
can be said to begin only with Maria Edgeworth's
Castle Rackrent, published in 1801. Miss Edgeworth was immediately concerned with social matters,
and her short book is a striking if highly coloured picture of the way of life of the decayed Anglo-Irish
gentry and their retainers.

During the nineteenth century, the heydey of the
novel as a popular form, other Irish writers emerged.
Among these only the works of William Carleton and
Gerald Griffin have survived in any way into this century. Admired by critics, both are still widely read by
the common reader. But writing as they were in the
earlier part of the century, both were concerned with
rural Ireland far removed from the urban life which
Joyce knew from childhood on. *The Black Prophet*
and *The Collegians,* powerful and curious though
they may be, are not models to be imitated by a
young writer whose experience of rural Ireland was
limited to a visit one summer to Mullingar. If Joyce
were to find models of urban literature, he had to
look elsewhere, hence his interest in European
writing.

Also these writers lacked a literary sense. They
wrote the open, rambling, loosely constructed novels
of their period. A tighter, more controlled feeling for
the construction and style of a novel was what concerned George Moore (1852-1933), arguably one of
the greatest of modern Irish writers, whose works are
only now, after a generation of neglect, beginning to
receive their just appraisal nearly fifty years after his
death.

Moore's life is a contrast to Joyce's. Born into a
wealthy national-minded Catholic family in Mayo,
George Moore came of class quite different to
Joyce's. He went to Paris to become a painter, and

failing in that, had settled to novel writing. It is hard now, I think, to appreciate the sensational nature of Moore's early work. He and Thomas Hardy were victims of banning by the influential circulating libraries of the day. Moore struck back with a stirring pamphlet *Literature at Nurse* in which he defended the right of the serious novelist to write as he chose.

Moore was influenced by the realism of the contemporary Russian and French writers. Having made his name with a series of realistic novels set in England, Moore returned to live in Dublin at the turn of the century, attracted by the possibilities of the Irish Revival for literature rather than for the poetic dreaminess which was all that Yeats and Russell seemed to be making of it. Though Moore's magnificent work *Hail and Farewell* was to provide the popular idea of the Revival and those involved in it (much to the chagrin of Yeats and Russell), he was not to have much influence on other writers around him, a brief lyrical outburst suiting the indolent Irish temperment more than a sustained prosaic narrative. There was one exception to this: James Joyce.

The direct influence of Moore on Joyce is clear enough — Joyce's stories of urban life followed quickly upon Moore's stories of rural life in *The Untilled Field*, the first of their kind. But because Moore was until recently 'unfashionable', it was an influence which few critics were keen to admit. Richard Ellmann refers, for instance, to *Vain Fortune* — the novel from which Joyce boldly lifted the celebrated ending of his story 'The Dead' — as a forgotten novel by George Moore. Forgotten it might have been in 1959, but in 1909 both the book and theme (which echoed events in Joyce's personal life) were still well known and admired.

What Moore was trying to do in the novels and stories he wrote in Ireland was to hold a mirror up to

Irish life in which the Irish could see themselves as
[122] they really were. In an earlier book, I have discussed
at greater length than is possible here the connections
between Joyce and Moore. Here I would only emphasise that what Moore only partially succeeded in
doing, Joyce triumphantly accomplished.

Moore's succcess was only partial because he fell in
with the prevailing notion of the Irish Revival that
the true Irish life was the life of rural Ireland. Joyce
did not believe this because his experience would not
let him. He had grown up in urban Ireland, and he
saw in the city the centre of paralysis which affected the whole country, affecting the moral and intellectual growth of the people.

Moore had brought into English literature the ideas
of a more genteel Zola. A novel demanded attention
to the details of life, moral and economic. Joyce continued this documentary approach to his fiction, as
the attention to detail in *Dubliners* and *Ulysses* attests.
Also by breaking with the last literary conventions
which had bound Moore, he was able to achieve a
more complete psychological picture of Irish life. But
such completeness, not only moral and economic, but
also sexual, brought with it the renewed threat of the
censor.

Joyce lived and worked outside Ireland during his
creative years. This meant that his influence was neg-
ligible for many years.

Writers of Yeats' generation were, as Joyce himself
observed, too old to be helped by him. Younger
writers of the generation of Frank O'Connor and Sean
O'Faolain were aware of Joyce. But they did not
follow his example, for their literary imaginations
were dominated not only by the influence of Russian
writers but also by a deadly dose of romanticism.
Joyce, as we have seen, had great difficulty with
Maunsels over the publication of *Dubliners*. This was

not due to fear on the firm's part, for a little later they were to bring out Brinsley MacNamara's bitter novel *The Valley of the Squinting Windows,* fully conscious of the controversy which it would arouse. But talented as he was, MacNamara was not a novelist in the same class as Joyce. Joyce aroused in Irish readers of that period a sense of fear which is now hard to recapture.

The Irish imagination runs to romanticism as a neglected garden runs to weed, or an ill-formed conscience to sin. The moral fibre of the country has been rotted by the evasions of reality that result from such a view of the world. It was this moral conscience that Joyce speaks of hammering out in the smithy of his soul in the closing passage of *A Portrait of the Artist.* The romantic view of life was repugnant to him. And so he was often repugnant to Irish readers.

Some influence on Flann O'Brien's pared language and domestic interiors, and paradoxically on Sean O'Casey's lushness in his autobiographies, can be detected towards the end of Joyce's life. But this was a mere matter of literary artifice, not of moral stance. Indeed respect for Joyce may, I think, well date only from the special memorial edition of the literary magazine *Envoy,* which John Ryan devoted to Joyce. Only then did Joyce as a writer rather than a literary legend begin to be widely appreciated in Ireland.

This appreciation was followed by a deepening influence. In the novels which John Broderick began to write in the latter part of the 1950s, and in the writings of John McGahern from the early 1960s, I can see the moral awareness of Joyce at work. *The Waking of Willie Ryan,* dealing with homosexuality, and *The Dark,* dealing with the sexual frustrations and ambitions of a rural youth, explored areas which were then regarded with great repugnance in Ireland. They were (of course) banned.

Joyce provides a stern model for any other writer. [124] He was not a professional author, turning out a book a year, to add to a shelf of works, eventually to make a collected edition in a uniform binding. Joyce attempted everything once, poetry, the *bildungsroman* ('novel of growth'), the novel, the drama, and whatever literary genre it is that *Finnegans Wake* belongs to. He tried, and achieved, a perfection of his ambitions in these forms. He had no desire to repeat himself. This constant striving to do something new makes him an heroic figure in literature. He is no journeyman. He is the master craftsman.

It is in this way that the life and work of Joyce continues to leaven the literature of modern Ireland. His significance in the moral history of the country will never lessen. In the letter quoted earlier to Grant Richards (see page 44), he spoke about 'the odour of ashpits' which hangs about his work. This is certainly true of the bleak scenes in *Dubliners*. But *Ulysses* is informed by a humorous humanity which is always refreshing. In the bleakness we can at this date easily recognise the landscape of modern Europe. But in Joyce's humanity, there is something more hopeful. And there, too, the significance of James Joyce is permanent. How little of this would have been understood by Joyce's friends when he left Dublin in 1904. How amazed they would have been!

12

Epilogue: Joyce's Dublin

Joyce's Dublin, that distant Dublin of dark Victorian nights and gay Edwardian days, is almost a lost world.

Ulysses presents the city as held in a perpetual stasis where it is always 16 June 1904, but the city itself has changed quite beyond Joyce's recognition. Before the last war, friends visiting Joyce in Paris could suggest the pervasive smell of petrol fumes as the only new feature in the city. Now the car has conquered all. Old landmarks, familiar shops and houses, even entire neighbourhoods have vanished.

The Martello Tower in Sandycove where *Ulysses* opens, and where Joyce himself spent only a very short time in 1904, is now a museum. They call it James Joyce's Tower, though it would have been more appropriate, seeing as how he paid the rent, to have called it Gogarty's Tower. But tourists are not interested in Gogarty. They want to see Joyce's cane and waistcoat, and the chair Sylvia Beach sat in. Nevertheless the place provides some sort of focus for foreigners interested in Joyce, with exhibitions, lectures and theatrical performances.

Many of the other settings of the novel have long gone, others remain almost unchanged. The school in Dalkey, where Joyce taught for a few months, and which is the setting of the second episode of the novel, is now let out in flats, a fate which has befallen many of the too large houses of the more ample-minded Victorian era. But the protean beach along which Stephen later walks into the city, and into eternity as he muses to himself, is much as it was, a wide desert of golden sand on hot summer mornings. But even here the tide brings in a deposit of filth and wreckage which tells in its own way the lesson of mutability which Stephen learnt here.

Change is not always protean. The residence of Mr Bloom, 7 Eccles Street, is now vanished, demolished along with much of the neighbourhood that Joyce knew in north Dublin, a victim of planner's blight, of civic indifference. This house had played a special role in Joyce's life, as well as providing (courtesy of J. F. Byrne) a home for the Blooms. The blue front door was removed by John Ryan, and now looms large in the interior of the Bailey in Duke Street — where Bloom refused to eat his lunch. Today he could not affort the place on his pittance.

Gone too are the wonderful Turkish Baths where Mr Bloom bathes — an unusual event in Dublin then, so Joyce claimed. This stood in minareted splendour opposite the rear entrance to Trinity College in Lincoln Place. Long unused, they have made way for a new building which has yet to be built. (One of the oddities of Joycean scholarship is its dependence on sources: it is now insisted that this place was not the Turkish Baths, though every Dubliner knows it was; the scholars prefer another house, where the offices of the owners were.)

Perhaps only the cemetery at Glasnevin remains very much as it was then: the monuments to the dead last longer in Dublin than the homes of the living. Gone too are the Ballast Office, Hely's in Dame Street, and Yeates' the occulists at the end of Grafton Street. Landmarks for generations, they have vanished in a few short years.

The newspaper office of the *Freeman's Journal* is now incorporated into the *Irish Independent,* a paper that still flourishes. However, when the film version of the novel was being made the director made use of [127] the offices of the *Irish Times*. But journalistic Dublin seems to have altered very little, as a brief visit to Bowes, with its mixed crowd of busmen and *Irish Times* writers will reveal, the blue jokes and the heated rhetoric in equal measure.

But other pubs and watering places in the novel, The Bailey, Davy Byrne's 'moral pub', are given over to a different crowd of young executives and their bored, well-bred girls. The Ship has closed, Barney Kiernan's is also gone, and the Ormonde where Bloom was enchanted by the siren music down on the quays has been reconstructed beyond recognition.

When Joyce was writing *Ulysses* he was anxious to have exact information. He would write back to his patient aunt in Dublin, and she would send out one of his nephews to ascertain whether the colour of the glass above some door was blue or red. Joyce explained once that he needed 'information about the Star of the Sea Church, has it ivy on its seafront, are there trees in Leahy's Terrace at the side or near, if so what? Are there steps leading down to the beach? I also want all the information you can give, tittle-tattle, facts etc. about Holles Street maternity hospital.'

There were steps: for this was where Bloom watches with rising excitement the two girls on the beach. But that scene is gone now, filled in to make way soon for a motorway. Some of the beach remains, providing now more ample views of girls that Mr Bloom (or Joyce himself) could have dreamt of. Holles St, which has an enviable reputation for the numbers of babies it brings into the world, still stands.

So too does the National Museum, though the Greek statues which stood around the foyer in all their naked splendour, were removed when Ireland got her independence. They were replaced by casts of Celtic [128] crosses. Across the way, in the National Library, much of the ambience of Joyce's day can still be savoured, though the desks have now been rearranged to discourage conversation and the flirtatious gossiping of the readers. Whether the earnest young Americans pouring over their critical editions fully appreciate the atmosphere is unlikely.

Gone too is the cabman's shelter in Beresford Place where Bloom and Stephen consume their coffee: another victim, like the site of Molly's bed, of changing times. Gone too the warren of streets a little way away, where the notorious red-light district stood. The houses themselves were closed in the 1920s, the girls reformed or hastened out of Ireland, the streets later demolished. But Dublin being Dublin, this being a 'poor area' has stayed a poor area, impoverished and crime ridden. The attitudes of the city fathers have not changed much in a hundred years.

But reading *Ulysses* one wonders about the girls who worked in the houses, those in Mrs Mack's who would have known Joyce: the country girls, Maud Russell, Jennie Bailey, Bridget Nagle, and the girls from over the water, Christina Gowly, Christina Purdy and Rose Thompson. Dead and gone. Only for ageing *literateurs* like Oliver Gogarty could these houses be shrouded in a golden glow; Joyce's view of nighttown as nightmare is closer to life. Like everything else in Ireland, even the trade has gone upmarket: the girls now work the expensive hotels on the south side.

Joyce had first explored these mean streets as a schoolboy at Belvedere, an institution that still flourishes. So too does his university, though it has long since outgrown the buildings on St Stephen's Green. However, a plaque on Newman's university now honours his name, and the learned members of the James Joyce Institute meet there in the winter to

resolve the conundrums of *Finnegans Wake*. Clongowes also survives in its remote fastness. Joyce's
homes, however, those endless little houses in North
Dublin in which the family struggled against vain fortune, strangely enough cling to existence. Leoville,
sans lion, sans stained glass, also stands, though bat-
tered and bewildered by a new highway that roars
past the back garden where little Jim played.

And the sea has done little in the passing years to
the house in Martello Terrace, where Joyce set the
scene of the Christmas dinner of 1891. And so back
by a circuitous vico of memory, through Castlewood Avenue, to Harold's Cross, to the house where
Joyce first encountered the image of his dark lady at
a children's party another Christmastime. And so to
the house in Brighton Square, now marked by yet
another plaque, where the infant first squirmed into
the long pain of his life that winter day of 1882.

Brighton Square has a timeless quality, where
people play tennis on summer evenings and children
chase each other in the autumn gloaming. But such
scenes vanish. Joyce's Dublin is now largely to be
found within his books. But the imaginative reader
may still find some interest in the life and world
through which Joyce passed.

Bibliography

The works of James Joyce
Stephen Hero (begun 1904; first published 1944)
Chamber Music (London 1907)
Dubliners (London 1914)
A Portrait of the Artist as a Young Man (New York 1916)
Exiles (London 1918)
Ulysses (Paris 1922)
Pomes Penyeach (Paris 1927)
Finnegans Wake (London 1939)

The Critical Writings of James Joyce, edited by Ellsworth Mason and Richard Ellmann (London 1959)
The Letters of James Joyce. Volume I, edited by Stuart Gilbert (London 1957); volumes II and III edited by Richard Ellmann (London 1966)
Selected Letters of James Joyce, edited by Richard Ellmann (London 1975); this volume includes previously unpublished letters.

Biographical works
Ellman, Richard, *James Joyce* (New York 1959)
Anderson, Chester G., *James Joyce and his world* (London 1967)
Beach, Sylvia, *Shakespeare and Company* (London 1960)

Budgen, Frank, *James Joyce and the Making of Ulysses* (London 1934)   [131]

Budgen, Frank, *Myselves When Young* (London 1970)

Colum, Mary and Padraic, *Our Friend James Joyce* (New York 1958)

Joyce, Stanislaus, *My Brother's Keeper* (London 1959)

Sullivan, Kevin, *Joyce Among the Jesuits* (New York 1958)

Some critical works

Burgess, Anthony, *Here Comes Everybody* (London 1965)

Campbell, Joseph and Henry Morton Robinson, *A Skeleton Key to Finnegans Wake* (New York 1944)

Goldberg, S. L., *The Classical Temper* (London 1961)

Goldberg, S. L., *James Joyce* (London 1962)

Gross, John, *James Joyce* (London 1971)

Litz, A. Walton, *James Joyce* (New York 1966)

Gilbert, Stuart, *James Joyce's Ulysses* (London 1930, 1952)

Tindall, William York, *A Reader's Guide to James Joyce* (London 1959)

Tindall, William York, *A Reader's Guide to Finnegans Wake* (London 1969)

Wilson, Edmund, *Axel's Castle* (New York 1931)

The number of books and articles now devoted to the works of Joyce are legion. The above are a very few titles which a reader unfamiliar with the unexplored hinterland may find of use in guiding him through the Joyce country.

On the city itself, the following might be read:

Hart, Clive, *A Topographical Guide to James Joyce's Ulysses* with maps by Leo Knuth (Colchester 1975)

Hutchins, Patricia, *James Joyce's Dublin* (Dublin 1950)

Hutchins, Patricia, *James Joyce's World* (London [132] 1957)

Pearl, Cyril, *Dublin in Bloomtime* (London 1969)

Tindall, William York, *The Joyce Country* (University Park, Pa. 1960)

More recent books on Joyce

Attridge, Derek, *The Cambridge Companion to James Joyce* (Cambridge 1990)

Bradley, Bruce, *James Joyce's Schooldays* (Dublin 1982)

Costello, Peter, *James Joyce: The Years of Growth* (London 1992)

Ellmann, Richard, *James Joyce* revised and enlarged edition (New York and London 1982)

Gifford, Don, *Joyce Annotated* (Berkeley and London 1982)

Gifford, Don, with Robert J. Sneidman, Ulysses *Annotated* (Berkeley and London 1988)

Igoe, Vivien, *James Joyce's Dublin Houses and Nora Barnacle's Galway* (Dublin 1997)

Jackson, John Wyse and Peter Costello, *John Stanislaus Joyce* (London 1997)

Jackson, John Wyse and Bernard McGinley, *James Joyce's* Dubliners. *An Annotated Edition* (London 1992)

Maddox, Brenda, *Nora: a Biography of Nora Joyce* (London 1988)

Nicholson, Robert, *The* Ulysses *Guide. Tours through Joyce's Dublin* (London 1988)

Pierce, David, *James Joyce's Ireland* (London 1992)

Potts, Willard (ed.), *Portraits of the Artist in Exile* (Dublin 1979)

Index

Adventures of Ulysses (Lamb), 13
Aquinas, Thomas, 14, 22
Aristotle, 14

Barnacle, Nora, *see* Joyce, Nora
Beach, Sylvia, 80, 87
Beatrice, 11
Beckett, Samuel, 88, 115
Belvedere College, 12, 18
Bodkin, Michael, 41, 49, 64
Broderick, John, 123
Budgen, Frank, 71, 73–5
Burton, Sir Richard, 42
Byrne, J. F., 19, 20, 52, 89, 126

Carleton, William, 120
censorship, 51, 64, 79, 87, 94
Cerf, Bennett, 93
Chamber Music (Joyce), 44, 46, 58, 75, 106
Christian Brothers, 12
cinema, 55–6
Clancy, George, 18, 19, 85
Clongowes Wood College, 8
Colum, Mary, 18, 91
Colum, Padraic, 18, 55, 65, 91
Conmee, Fr John, 9
Conway, Mrs, 7
Cosgrave, Vincent, 18, 26, 30, 37, 44, 52
Curran, C. P., 2, 4, 17, 30, 35, 97

Dante, 11, 18, 65, 119
Darlington, Fr Joseph, 17
'The Dead' (Joyce), 48–50
de Valera, E., 6
'Drama and Life' (Joyce), 20
Dubliners (Joyce), 31, 44, 51, 62, 107–9

'Ecce Puer' (Joyce), 91
Edgeworth, Maria, 120

Eliot, T. S., 101, 106, 119
Ellmann, Richard, 3, 14, 45, 121
Envoy, 123
'Et Tu, Healy' (Joyce), 11
Exiles (Joyce), 66–68

Finnegans Wake (Joyce), 2, 6, 20, 31, 57, 87, 94–104, 111–12, 114
Fleischmann, Helen, *see* Joyce, Helen
Fleischmann, Martha, 74
Franck, Nino, 100
Freeman's Journal, 31, 126
Freund, Gisèle, 4, 105

Gaelic League, 20
Gas from a Burner (Joyce), 65
Giacomo Joyce (Joyce), 57, 66, 75
Giedion, Prof. and Mrs, 117
Gogarty, Oliver St John, 32, 35, 37, 52, 85, 125
Gonne, Maud, 26
Gorman, Herbert, 12, 86, 116
Gregory, Augusta Lady, 24–6
Griffin, Gerald, 120
Griffith, Arthur, 109, 119

Healy, Tim, 10
Holy Office, The (Joyce), 35
Hopkins, G. M., 17
Huebsch, Ben, 69, 75
Human Personality (Myers), 29

Ibsen, Henrik, 18, 20, 119
Imagists, 106
Irish Homestead, 24, 31, 35
Irish language, 20
Irish Times, 88, 127

Jesuits, 9, 22
Jolas, Eugene, 86, 91

Jolas, Maria, 91, 115
Joyce, Eileen, 61, 62
Joyce, Eva, 54, 61
Joyce, George, 43, 51, 85, 95—6, 101, 117
Joyce, Helen, 90, 91, 96
Joyce, James Augustine,
    Knowledge of, 1
    avocations of, 2,
    themes of, 3, 112
    appearance, 3,
    childhood, 6
    parents, 8
    education, 9—13
    reading, 13
    early writings, 14, 21—3
    literary vocation, 15
    at university, 16ff
    in Paris, 25
    mother dies, 26—8
    first stories, 29—40
    meets wife, 33
    on his early life, 36
    leaves Ireland, 39
    in Trieste, 41ff
    birth of son, 43
    publishing difficulties, 44, 51ff
    Chamber Music published, 46
    Dubliners, 48—60
    emotional crisis, 51—60
    cinema manager, 55—6
    explicit letters, 57—60
    life in Trieste, 61—3
    Dubliners rejected, 64
    Exiles written, 66—8
    Ulysses begun, 69
    first books, 68—9
    in Zurich, 68ff
    work on *Ulysses*, 73—83
    in Paris, 79ff
    Work in Progress, 84ff
    Ulysses in America, 86, 93
    family life, 87—93
    marriage, 90
    Ulysses in Britain, 93
    Ulysses in Ireland, 94
    daughter's illness, 98ff
    Finnegans Wake, 98ff
    Joyce the writer, 105ff
    Finnegans Wake published, 114
    leaves Paris, 115
    in Zurich, 116
    last illness, 117—18
    death 119,
    significance of life, 119ff

and Irish literature, 120—4
and Dublin, 124—9
Joyce, John Stanislaus, 8, 9, 23, 25, 28, 91
Joyce, Lucia, 63, 89, 92, 95—9, 101, 115, 116
Joyce, May Murray, 8, 23, 27—8
Joyce, Nora, 33ff, 51, 52—60, 84—5, 87—90, 101, 102
Joyce, P. W., 77
Joyce, Stanislaus, 8, 45, 51, 62
Joyce, Stephen, 91, 115

Kettle, Thomas, 18

Lamb, Charles, 13
Lane, Allen, 93
Le Brocquy, Louis, 4
Lenin, V.I., 71
Léon, Paul, 88
Lever, Charles, 42
Little Review, 75, 79

McCormack, John, 32, 35
McCormack, Mrs, 71, 78
McGahern, John, 123
MacNamara, Brinsley, 123
Matthews, Elkin, 65
Maunsels, 47, 51, 62, 64—5, 122
Modern Movement, 118
Monnier, Adrienne, 80
Montague, John, 4
Moore, George, 24, 120—2
moral history of Ireland, 44, 124
Myers, F. H., 29
My Brother's Keeper (Joyce), 45

Newman, John Henry, Cardinal, 17, 128

O'Brien, Flann, 123
O'Casey, Sean, 114, 123
O'Connor, Frank, 122
O'Faolain, Sean, 122
Osservatore Romano, 14, 88

Parnell, C. S., 10—11
Pearse, Patrick, 20, 113
Phillips, Stephen, 17
'Portrait of the Artist' (Joyce, essay), 30
Portrait of the Artist as a Young Man (Joyce, novel), 15, 39, 46, 69, 108—109
Pound, Ezra, 68, 72, 78, 106, 118

Power, Arthur, 105, 113
Prezioso, Roberto, 62, 66

Reddin, Kenneth, 2
religion, 13, 22–3, 91, 119
Revival, Irish, 20, 47, 113, 119, 121
Richards, Grant, 44, 75, 124
Roberts, George, 51, 64–5
Russell, George, 24, 31, 109, 121
Ryan, John, 123, 126

Shaw, G. B., 54
Sketflngton, Francis, 18, 21, 85
Stephen Hero (Joyce), 45, 69
Straumann, Heinrich, 116–17
Sullivan, John, 92
Sullivan, Kevin, 14
Sykes, Mr and Mrs, 72
Symons, Arthur, 26
Synge, J. M., 27, 47, 72
syphilis, 28

Transatlantic Review, 86
transition, 86
Tuohy, Patrick, 2
Tzara, Tristan, 71

Ulysses (Joyce), 2, 6, 29, 52, 57, 67–71, 73, 110
Ulysses (Phillips), 18
University College Dublin, 14–17
Untilled Field, The (Moore), 121

Vain Fortune (Moore), 121
Vance, Eileen, 7
Volta cinema, 55–6

Weaver, Harriet, 69, 70–71, 84, 94, 97, 115
Wells, H. G., 70
Woolf, Virginia, 100
Woolsey, J. M., 93
Work in Progress (Joyce), 86, 114

Yeats, W. B., 19, 22, 25, 46, 85, 113, 119, 121

AN ILLUSTRATED
HISTORY OF
IRELAND

John Grenham

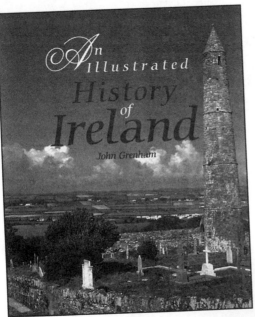

An *Illustrated History of Ireland* provides a fascinating account of the origins of the Irish people from prehistoric times to the present day. It tells of the effect of invasion, war, famine and emigration and how these have influenced the make up of Ireland and the Irish.

Illustrated throughout with full-colour photographs of landscapes, historic sites and artefacts, this book will be welcomed by Irish people at home and abroad.

| £5.99 | PAPERBACK | 0 7171 2553 X |